MARCUS AURELIUS IN LOVE

T0308980

Marcus Aurelius in Love

Marcus Aurelius & Marcus Cornelius Fronto

EDITED, TRANSLATED, AND WITH
AN INTRODUCTION AND
COMMENTARY BY
AMY RICHLIN

*

The University of Chicago Press   Chicago & London

The University of Chicago Press, Chicago 60637
The University of Chicago Press, Ltd., London
© 2006 by The University of Chicago
All rights reserved. Published 2006.
Paperback edition 2016
Printed in the United States of America

25 24 23 22 21 20 19 18 17 16   2 3 4 5 6

ISBN-13: 978-0-226-71300-7 (cloth)
ISBN-13: 978-0-226-37811-4 (paper)
ISBN-13: 978-0-226-71302-1 (e-book)
DOI: 10.7208/chicago/9780226713021.001.0001

Library of Congress Cataloging-in-Publication Data

Marcus Aurelius, Emperor of Rome, 121–180.
    Marcus Aurelius in love / Marcus Aurelius and Marcus Cornelius Fronto ;
edited, translated, and with an introduction and commentary by Amy Richlin.
        p. cm.
    Includes bibliographical references and index.
    ISBN-13: 978-0-226-71300-7 (cloth : alk. paper)
    ISBN-10: 0-226-71300-8 (cloth : alk. paper)
        1. Marcus Aurelius, Emperor of Rome, 121–180—Correspondence.
    2. Fronto, Marcus Cornelius—Correspondence. 3. Love letters—Rome.
    I. Marcus Aurelius, Emperor of Rome, 121–180. Correspondence II. Fronto,
    Marcus Cornelius. III. Richlin, Amy, 1951– IV. Title.
    PA6389.F7A4 2006
    188—dc22

                                                                    2006011165

⊗ This paper meets the requirements of ANSI/NISO Z39.48-1992
(Permanence of Paper).

Dear Lon

Contents

Acknowledgments

First of all I must thank Clifford Ando, who said, after a lecture I gave in Toronto on sentimental friendships in the circle of Cicero, "If you want to see a sentimental friendship, look at the letters of Fronto." I took his advice, and voilà.

This project was made possible by a fellowship from the American Council of Learned Societies in 2003–4, without which it would have been much delayed; I am deeply grateful. The project funded was in fact a scholarly book on Cornelius Fronto and his relationship with his imperial pupil, the young Marcus Aurelius, which I hope will follow hard on the heels of this one. But it was the archival work I was able to do in the summer of 2003 that showed me what a good thing it would be to make the Marcus and Fronto letters widely available in a new translation. The incomparable facilities of the ONE National Gay and Lesbian Archives in Los Angeles opened my eyes to issues concerning the circulation of knowledge about ancient sexuality, and I thank Ashlie Mildfelt, Joseph Hawkins, and especially Stuart Timmons for their patience, good humor, and endless willingness to fill in blanks with their knowledge of a living tradition. Special tribute is due to the ghosts of Jim Kepner and W. Dorr Legg, which hover benignly over the archive they created.

Helen Morales graciously invited me to come talk about Fronto at Cambridge in the spring of 2004, thus tumbling me into another great collection; many thanks to the staff at the Classical Faculty

Library, especially Stephen Howe, to Newnham College for its hospitality, and to William Fitzgerald for motivating me to finish up. In London, Rictor Norton was kind enough to meet with me to talk about the Victorians and underground scholarship, and his honesty and courage as a scholar have been an inspiration.

In the summer and fall of 2005, I was fortunate enough to receive advice from two experts in the early modern. Christoph Leidl corrected my forays into German literary criticism and contributed generously to my ongoing work on Fronto in the nineteenth century. David M. Robinson read the letters and shone the light of his knowledge of eighteenth-century style on letters 2 and 3. Remaining errors are all mine.

Douglas Mitchell at the University of Chicago Press gave Marcus and Fronto the warm welcome they've been awaiting for almost two hundred years. It's a pleasure to deal with an editor whose sense of humor is as acute as his sense of history, whose (electronic) letters I always look forward to reading, and whose unfailing kindness and courtesy kept the book moving painlessly forward. All the Chicago staff, notably Tim McGovern and Christine Schwab, were wonderful; Joseph Brown completed the meticulous copyedit in Hammond, Louisiana, during Hurricane Katrina.

To my former colleagues and students in the Classics Department at the University of Southern California, who managed to soldier on without me in 2003–4 while I wallowed in epistolography, my gratitude as always—and particularly to Clifford Ando for help with the notes, and to William G. Thalmann, who was kind enough to purge the Greek letters of their worst faults. Lisl Walsh, research assistant extraordinaire, kept things organized while I moved to UCLA, where I benefited from the erudition of my new colleagues Shane Butler, Sander Goldberg, Robert Gurval, and Michael Haslam. Mark Masterson, Philip Purchase, and James Tatum each provided conversation, exhortation, and epistolary stimulation at key points along the way—especially the divine Tatum, who, with Joseph Boone, David Konstan, and the redoubtable Mary Beard, gave essential support to the project. It owes a lot to their work on masculinity, friendship, and letter writing and to Tatum's fatal charm and relentless cruelty as a coach. Molly Myerowitz Levine provided vital help, with her usual openhearted generosity. Most of all I thank and mourn for the late Jonathan Walters, who let me raid his library, patiently answered a million questions, schlepped to the British Library for me, and put up with more Fronto Facts in a day than any one person should have to listen to, and whose deep knowledge of the tradition of homoerotic writing helped me see what I was doing. *Tam cari capitis.*

But this book of love letters is dedicated to the one I love. I wrote most of it far from home, looking up from the page to the blue Pacific, and thinking, with Marcus, *Quid mihi tecum est? Amo absentem.*

Introduction

In 1815 Angelo Mai found a long-lost treasure of the classical world in the Ambrosian Library in Milan: a palimpsest codex containing, among other works, many of the letters of Marcus Cornelius Fronto and his correspondents, who included the emperor Marcus Aurelius. News of the discovery was greeted with joy, for Fronto was then known only by his ancient reputation as an orator in a class with Cicero, and Marcus Aurelius was the revered author of the book now known as the *Meditations*. Mai was a great palimpsest hunter, and, by an amazing coincidence, when he was transferred to the Vatican Library in 1818, he found there part of the same codex, containing another large section of the Fronto letters. A *codex* is just a book—the Latin term was coined in antiquity to distinguish texts in this form from those in the earlier format, the book roll. A *palimpsest* is a parchment page that has been recycled—written on once, washed and reused for a second text, and then, as here, bound into a new codex. The trick is to read past the overlying text to the precious, more ancient text below it.

Mai duly did so, but when he published the first text in 1815 and the combined results in 1823, the cries of joy turned to howls of dismay. The long-awaited Fronto was not at all what his nineteenth-century audience had expected, and his reputation immediately sank to a low that has persisted for almost two hundred years and kept most scholars from paying any attention to him at all. The letters are widely supposed to be extremely boring and badly written, and critics from the early nineteenth century to the present have said that it would have been better for Fronto's reputation if they had never been found. Almost no one was interested in the content of the letters, and their main value was often said to lie in the fondness of Fronto and his correspondents for quoting from early Latin literature: the letters were read as a ragbag of otherwise lost scraps of more highly esteemed authors.

Mai, meanwhile, was widely reviled for the quality of his first published edition. Moreover, using the technology available to him, Mai had treated the Ambrosian palimpsest with chemicals that gradually—according to the few people ever allowed to set eyes on it—made it illegible altogether. And he kept the manuscripts under tight control until his death in 1854. His edition became a popular playground for a favorite sport of nineteenth-century Classics: conjectural emendation. That is, relying on their familiarity with the ways of scribes and on the excellence of their own knowledge of Latin, scholars would guess what the original text must have said. Optimally, the process of restoring an ancient text—known as *textual criticism*—involves comparing all available manuscripts, deciding which are most reliable, and extrapolating the wording of the original. In this case, all there was to go on was Mai's word for what he had seen in the manuscripts; the second-guessing began as early as 1816, with an edition organized by B. G. Niebuhr. After Mai's death a few others did try to decipher the manuscripts anew, and the classical press Teubner published a new edition by Samuel Naber in 1867, which was itself not viewed as perfect, leading to more conjectures. Edmund Hauler then devoted a long career to poring over the manuscripts and publishing small corrections, piecemeal, in scholarly journals, always looking forward to the eventual grand new edition that never appeared. In the mid-twentieth century, Michael van den Hout took up the work, bringing out a new Teubner edition in 1988 and the first-ever commentary on the letters in 1999. Van den Hout was able to make use of Hauler's notes, though he confides at the beginning of the Teubner that this made his job no easier (1988, vii). Much of van den Hout's text and commentary is taken up with further—and still inconclusive—textual emendations, and the text and notes to the translation you hold in your hands reflect this state of things: this is a translation of a text with places in it that flicker like an old neon sign. The Fronto letters do not even have a standard numbering system, hence the bulky references used here (see the concordance for an explanation).

Readers should also note that even what Mai found was not the complete text, but was missing about 43 percent of the original whole; that the recycled pages were jumbled, a major problem in understanding the text; that, within what Mai found, there were gaps; and that the original itself would have been a selection, although by whom it was made and when in antiquity the collection was published are questions that remain mysterious. It is clear that the letters were never widely known and may have existed even in late antiquity in only a very few copies.

So far we see the letters found and yet, to a large extent, still hidden. How were they to reach a larger audience? The first translation into English was done in 1824 by J. McQuige, in Rome, although only of some of the letters; a translation into French of the whole collection was made in 1830 by Armand Cassan. A few scholars incorporated translations of some letters into books about Marcus Aurelius or (a very few) about Fronto. The first translation into English of the whole collection did not appear until 1919–20—the Loeb Classical Library translation of C. R. Haines, in two volumes. Haines had previously done the Loeb edition of the *Meditations* of Marcus Aurelius, but he was not otherwise a well-known scholar. Like other Loeb editors, including the great W. H. D. Rouse, he was a schoolteacher. The Loeb editions carry the Latin or Greek on the left-hand page and the English translation on the facing page; although they were aimed at bringing the classics to the general public and are available in most big public libraries, this format seems to keep them from achieving a wide readership. Haines's edition not only provided an honest, word-for-word translation but also included good notes and made a number of sensible emendations. And there it has sat on the library shelves for almost a century.

Well, why should anybody have paid attention? Fronto's ancient reputation, well-known to the classically educated Victorians, was a matter of no interest to the scientific twentieth century. Today, however, Fronto may be starting to look more interesting. To begin with, he was an African, from Cirta in Numidia (now Constantine, Algeria). His name is Roman, and he came from a wealthy family, but his actual ethnicity is unknown. He may belong to the colonizers, and he may just as well come of local stock; in letter 21 of this collection, he famously describes himself as "a Libyan of the Libyan nomads." How literally he means this is one of the many mysteries that surround the letters, but his biographer thinks he probably did have indigenous ancestors (Champlin 1980, 8). In any case, he came to Rome to make his fortune and rose to become the foremost orator of his time. Owing to this reputation, in 139 CE he was chosen to instruct the young Marcus Aurelius, the future emperor, in rhetoric. And—what is now, finally, a matter of scholarly interest— maybe they fell in love.

Marcus Aurelius was born on April 26, 121 CE; the short form of his given name would have been Marcus Annius, and he came to be called Marcus Annius Verus. A child when his father died, he was raised by his mother, the heiress Domitia Lucilla, in the house of his father's father until he was almost seventeen. In January of 138 the emperor Hadrian, nearing the end of his life, adopted Marcus's uncle, Titus Aurelius Antoninus, as his son and successor, and brought Marcus to live with him. At the same time, he instructed Antoninus to adopt Marcus as *his* son and successor, at which time Marcus became Marcus Aurelius Verus. (Marcus was to change his name one last time on the death of Pius in 161, when he became the emperor Marcus Aurelius Antoninus.) After Hadrian died in July of 138, Marcus's uncle became the emperor Antoninus Pius and Marcus received the additional name of Caesar. In 139 Pius chose Fronto, then in his mid-forties, as Marcus's teacher.

The events of Marcus's life are known mostly through much later sources, of which the best are the *Historia Augusta* biographies of Hadrian, Antoninus Pius, and Marcus and a very late condensed version of book 70 of Cassius Dio's history, all of them full of inconsistencies and garblings. Extant coins from the period help with the name changes. The *Historia Augusta* (*HA*) itself adds another layer of mystery to the story. The *Historia Augusta* pretends to be a multiauthored set of lives of the emperors written around 300 CE; scholars now agree that it was actually produced by a single writer working around 400 CE and that its truth-value is often dubious. When, in this translation, a note refers to the *HA Life of Marcus,* it is talking about the biography of Marcus in the *Historia Augusta* (for a translation, see Birley 1976, 108–37). The *Historia Augusta* writer loves scandal and gossip of all kinds; he has plenty to say about the goings-on in the house of Hadrian and about the incredible behavior of Marcus Aurelius's son Commodus—much watered-down in the movie *Gladiator* (Ridley Scott, 2000). The *Life of Marcus* does mention Fronto as one of Marcus's teachers. It does not say that Marcus and Fronto were lovers.

In Roman aristocratic culture, it was a commonplace to insult an opponent by claiming that he had been sexually used by an adult male in his youth (see Richlin 1993, 538). Suetonius's biographies of the emperors and the *Historia Augusta* are full of such stories, which never provide corroborating evidence. You would expect stories like this for Marcus too, but there are none. Meanwhile, the letters between Marcus and Fronto from 139 to 145, when Marcus married Pius's daughter Faustina, provide what appears to be direct evidence of a living relationship of some kind. The letters do not seem to have been written with an eye to publication, as some ancient letters do; except for a few clearly marked as such, they are not literary compositions, and they are far removed from the imaginary letters then popular, which are like prose poems (see Costa 2001; Rosenmeyer 2001). They speak of everyday life and common acquaintances; in this, they are much like the numerous extant letters of Cicero, which Fronto admired, and of the younger Pliny (see Ebbeler 2002). It might be argued that their eroticism is self-conscious, knowingly in the tradition of other letter exchanges, as Erik Gunderson argues for Pliny (1997; cf. Richlin 1992, 34). They definitely do not seem to be forgeries, of which there are plenty in antiquity—some in the *Historia Augusta.* Forgeries basically say what you would expect the writer to say—they are a form of historical fiction—while the Marcus-Fronto letters by no means say what is expected. The future emperor, revered as a sort of saint from antiquity onward, is exuberant, slangy, sometimes impudent, and (as he says himself in letter 37) bubbling over with love for Fronto; the eminent orator responds cautiously but, in the end, with a tragic sense of desertion and betrayal. Their correspondence was to continue to the end of Fronto's life, but much changed.

Were Marcus and Fronto in love? Were they lovers? *Marcus Aurelius in Love* presents only a selection of letters: all the letters from the years 139–48 (but see below on dating) that testify to the feelings of the correspondents. Very few of the few scholars who have read the letters at all have ventured to say that they are love letters: John Boswell, in a footnote to *Christianity, Social Tolerance, and Homosexuality* (1980, 134 n. 40), was one; Robert Boughner, in a talk given at a meeting of the American Philological Association in 1990, was another. Discussion of the emotional aspects of the letters often depends on two generalizations: (1) personal discourse in the second century CE was flowery and routinely expressed extreme devotion as a polite matter of form; (2) other historical periods defined *friendship* differently from the way we do today, and forms of *sentimental friendship* have existed that involved romantic mutual devotion but not necessarily physical expression. Such relationships are especially familiar from the nineteenth century, and scholars know them well from the work of Alan Bray (*The Friend*), Linda Dowling (*Hellenism and Homosexuality in Victorian Oxford*), Lillian Faderman (*Surpassing the Love of Men*), and Eve Kosofsky Sedgwick (*Between Men*), among others. I do not expect all, or even most, readers of this collection to be convinced that Marcus and Fronto were lovers. What I hope is that these remarkable letters will be rescued from oblivion, that historians of ancient sexuality will take a good look at them, that Marcus Aurelius's halo will be knocked a little awry, and that to Fronto will be restored some of the credit due him as a writer.

I also hope that these letters will be of interest to those students of gay history who still value the quest for ancestors. When I looked to see whether the letters, so despised by the scholarly establishment, might have been noticed and picked up by various homophile writers of the nineteenth and twentieth centuries, I found that they had not been: surprising, when so much else *was* noticed. Edward Carpenter, for example, the eminent Edwardian radical, put together in his *Ioläus* (1902) a sort of canon of exemplars of male-male love from antiquity but said nothing of these letters. The more influential John Addington Symonds, in his *A Problem in Greek Ethics* (1883; see Norton 1997), wrote so damningly of Roman male-male love as opposed to Greek that subsequent generations of homophile writers have been unable to see much worthy of respect or interest in Roman texts. Underground magazines of the mid-twentieth century like *Der Weg zu Freundschaft, Der Kreis/Le Cercle, ONE,* and the *Mattachine Review* cycle through the same short list of ancient models: David and Jonathan, Achilles and Patroclus, the Theban Band, Alexander and Hephaistion, and Hadrian and Antinoüs (see Richlin 2005). Interestingly, in a usage that goes back at least to the notorious conclusion of Walter Pater's *Studies in the History of the Renaissance* (1873, orig. 1868), the word *friend* had acquired for this group almost a code meaning of "lover." For such readers, the repeated use of *amicus,* "friend," and its cognates by Marcus and Fronto would not have precluded the inference of an erotic relationship. But, of them all, only Pater shows signs of having set eyes on the Marcus-Fronto letters; he made the (overly) aged Fronto and the middle-aged Marcus into characters in his riddling novel *Marius the Epicurean* (1885). It is thought-provoking to consider that Pater wrote this novel to retract the (anti-Christian? homophile?) views that had caused him so much trouble in his book of essays, and that his career was thwarted by the famous Benjamin Jowett, translator of Plato, on the basis of love letters between himself and an Oxford student, William Money Hardinge (see Inman 1991).

Another factor that might have inhibited the reading of the Marcus-Fronto letters as erotic is the widespread cult of Marcus Aurelius as a saintly hero, in full swing in the nineteenth century (e.g., Niebuhr 1843) and continuing on into the present. This cult is based on Marcus Aurelius's book known as the *Meditations*—its actual title seems to have been *To Himself*—which is itself a somewhat mysterious text, written in an odd and difficult Greek, and which seems to have been very little known in antiquity, not even referred to until the fourth century CE, and rarely thereafter. Composed late in Marcus's life, and consisting largely of thoughts on ethics based on Stoicism, this book includes, in its first section, a sort of moral autobiography.

This autobiography is relevant here for two reasons. First, it begins with a list of people to whom the writer is grateful, and the reasons why. Among these people are teachers, and to readers of the letters it is a particularly poignant fact that Fronto is mentioned eleventh in the list, and only for having taught the writer to esteem the quality of *philostorgia*, "warmheartedness" (a quality prized by the Stoics as the foundation of an ethical upbringing; see Gaca 2003, 81). Second, the writer does include a few details about his personal sexual ethics, among which are (1) that his (adoptive) father had set him an example by having "overcome all passion for boys," (2) that "I preserved the flower of my youth, and . . . did not make proof of my virility before the proper season," and (3) that "I never touched Benedicta or Theodotus" (1.16–17; Long's translation). These entirely negative claims seem to be responsible for the occasional mentions of Marcus Aurelius in the popular tradition of homophile ancestors.

I hope this little translation, then, will open up a conversation. There is no other extant collection of love letters from antiquity, much less a pederastic one; I said myself in print (1992, 38, 55–56; 1993, 539), before reading the Marcus-Fronto letters, that the boy's side of such a relationship is unattested, the power of speech being reserved for the adult male. Of course a relationship between a future emperor and his teacher cannot have been normative. But these letters provide a complex version of the shadings of power within a relationship and of the interconnections of love with other Roman systems: family, pedagogy, rhetoric, philosophy, literature, sex/gender, body, history. And, as James Zetzel (2000) remarks: "For Fronto it is an almost erotic attachment to the Latin language itself that produces his most overpowering writing."

The general reader, for whom this book is written, might want an orientation to some norms of Roman society during the second century CE.

History

Rome began as a kingdom, so stories told, in 753 BCE, and from 510 BCE went on as a republic; but around 31 BCE, after a hundred years of civil war, the youthful Gaius Julius Caesar Octavianus, the last strongman left standing after a brutal series of duels, became the first emperor, later known as Augustus, and the republic came to an end. Augustus's adoptive father and predecessor, Julius Caesar, his ten successors, and he form the subjects of Suetonius's well-known set of biographies of emperors; they constitute the first two Roman dynasties, the Julio-Claudians and the Flavians, the latter coming to an end in 96 CE. Suetonius, however, wrote under the third dynasty, carrying on a familiar Roman tradition of writing about what was safely dead. This third dynasty, the Antonines, takes us into the later years of the second century CE: Nerva, Trajan, Hadrian, Antoninus Pius, Marcus Aurelius, Commodus. Except for the father-son pair of Marcus Aurelius and Commodus, the succession was achieved through adoption, a policy that Marcus Aurelius should probably have followed himself.

With the fall of the republic and the concentration of political power in the hands of one man, the Roman upper class, which produced most of the texts we have, had lost its ancestral raison d'être: the rule of Rome and its provinces. Where rhetoric for Roman elite men had once been only a means to political power, now the mastery of rhetoric became an end in itself—a source of prestige. Yet at the same time all public speech was now charged with fear, a situation epitomized by the fate of the greatest republican orator, Cicero: his head and right hand were displayed on the Rostra in the Forum along with the heads of other victims of the bloodbath that inaugurated Augustus's rise to power (see Richlin 1999; Butler 2002). And successive emperors made it clear that eminent men needed to watch their mouths—indeed, they had many senators executed and forced others to suicide. We find in the younger Pliny—another letter writer and orator and Fronto's coeval—a classic performance of the senator's predicament, at that point in his eighty-page panegyric speech to the emperor Trajan where he says: "You command us to be free, and we will be; you command us to disclose what we feel: we will disclose it" (*Panegyricus* 66.4). Hadrian's reign began and ended with killings (*HA Life of Hadrian* 7.1–4, 23.1–9), and, although Antoninus Pius was a kinder, gentler emperor (*HA Life of Antoninus Pius* 7.2–3, 8.10), at the beginning of his reign it would have been impossible to be sure. Fronto would certainly have known he had to be very careful.

Sex and Gender

The Greek and Roman sex/gender systems have been the subject of much discussion in the past twenty years or so, and readers may already be familiar with writings by Bernadette Brooten, K. J. Dover, Michel Foucault, David Halperin, Thomas Hubbard, Craig Williams, and John J. Winkler. (Suggestions for further background reading are offered at the end of the introduction.) Writers from the fifth and fourth centuries BCE in classical Greece, especially Athens, portray a system in which women are stereotyped as either good wives or adulteresses, respectable women or whores. Female-female sexuality is rarely mentioned (see Brooten 1996). Adult males were normally expected to be attracted both to women and to adolescent males, roughly between the ages of twelve and eighteen; the adult male is called the *erastês* (lover), the boy the *erômenos* (beloved). This active/passive nomenclature corresponds to some degree to sexual behavior, the adult male pursuing and penetrating, the boy pursued and penetrated. This institution is known as *pederasty,* from the Greek *paiderastia,* "boy love"; readers should realize that these boys were not considered children and that ancient pederasty is a different concept from modern pedophilia. Meanwhile, adult males who wished to be penetrated by other men were mocked—most commonly as *kinaidoi* or *euruprôktoi* (wide-assholed)—and men used accusations of such behavior against their opponents in court cases and other competitive situations.

The penetrator/penetrated model is much more clearly attested for later periods (on classical Greece, see Davidson 1997, 2001; Hubbard 1998). Romans achieved political hegemony over most of the Mediterranean by 146 BCE, and the word *Rome* is today used to refer both to the indigenous cultures of Italy and to Greek, Semitic, and other cultures from all over the Mediterranean and Western Europe under Roman rule; it is not possible to separate out these cultural strands after the first century BCE or so. The later the period, the more texts we have. So, as we get into the periods dominated by Rome, we have much more comedy, gossip, and invective, and also more legal sources, than we have for the period of Plato, in classical Greece (see Richlin 1992). This is partly what accounts for what John Addington Symonds perceived as the comparative coarseness of Roman culture.

What these sources make clear is that, for Romans, the sex/gender system was integrated with the institution of slavery; the only permissible adolescent male sex object in Roman law was a slave, and, indeed, slaves were generally considered the sexual property of their owners. However, it is also clear that, as always, love was no respecter of rules, and that free Roman male adolescents were sex objects, if dangerous ones—jailbait, as it were (not that the Romans had jails). Roman law made the rape, seduction, or sexual harassment of adolescent male citizens a crime, or at least a tort. Moreover, it imposed civil penalties on any free male who allowed the "womanish" use of his body (see Richlin 1993). Males past adolescence who continued to want to play the boy's part were socially stigmatized and served as an unfailing source of humor and invective, in which they are most commonly called *cinaedi* (from Greek *kinaidoi*) or *molles* (soft).

Basically, then, the free adolescent male in this system is assimilated to slaves and women, both of which were considered degraded classes in Greco-Roman cultures, and pederastic relationships were therefore always fraught with a certain tension between idealization and shame. The second century CE, when Marcus and Fronto lived, offers many texts in which pederasty plays a key role; notable are several literary debates on the relative merits of sex with women as opposed to sex with boys: Plutarch's *Erôtikos,* pseudo-Lucian's *Erôtes,* and a section of the novel *Leucippe and Clitophon,* by Achilles Tatius (see Halperin 1992; Winkler 1989).

Literature

Love poetry in antiquity written by men—that is, almost all extant love poetry—dealt equally with women and with boys from its earliest traces in archaic Greece. Latin literature grew up alongside a flourishing Greek tradition of erotic epigrams (short poems in couplets), and Romans wrote their own, in Latin and Greek, from the second century BCE on; for instances in which the Marcus-Fronto letters intersect with that tradition, see letters 14 and 44. Moreover, poets of the first century BCE fostered a Roman tradition of love poetry whose language is so distinctive that it has a name, the *sermo amatorius*—"lover's speech." The Marcus-Fronto letters are full of this amatory vocabulary; intriguingly, they often echo the poems of Catullus, whose name they never mention, though they cite so many others.

Catullus (d. 55 BCE) is of particular interest here because of the way in which he makes writing into a homosocial activity shared among a group of close male friends—erudite, politically savvy, upper-class, urbane (i.e., hip to the city of Rome). He writes poems about writing poems, about swapping words with his friends in an exchange that is both competitive and erotic; in this he sets the mode for later poets (see Oliensis 1997). From Catullus through Sidonius Apollinaris in the fifth century CE, these exchanges are set at dinner parties, which thereby become the social occasion for the meeting of literary men. The elegist Propertius, the lyric poet Horace, the satirist Persius, the letter writer Pliny—all set their writing in a network of men. And among them towers the orator Cicero, Catullus's contemporary, who himself shows up in Catullus's poems—and who, Pliny says in a letter, wrote an erotic poem to his (male) slave, Tiro (Richlin 1992, 34, 223; Beard 2002). Latin literature is always about itself as well as about its ostensible subject; the mistresses addressed by the elegists are today understood as *scriptae puellae,* "written girls," and the same could be said of Catullus's Juventius, Tibullus's Marathus, Horace's Lycidas, and so on. They are like pinups; the poems about them are erotic objects in themselves.

Pederastic love poetry always existed alongside a parallel tradition of invective, which, indeed, outlasted it. Not only the formal genre of satire but a great deal of lyric poetry and epigram took delight in attacking the figure of the *kinaidos/mollis.* In Greece as well as in Rome, these literary forms had lowly popular-culture cousins — taunts, graffiti, caricatures, farce — as well as high-toned cousins in history, biography, rhetoric, and technical writing (medicine, law, astronomy, physiognomy). In all these forms, both the desired beautiful boy and the reviled *mollis* man are familiar figures.

The Marcus-Fronto letters, then, as texts, have these parallel traditions as their context. When Marcus and Fronto write of themselves as each other's *erastês*—when Fronto writes to Herodes Atticus that he is Herodes' *anterastês* (see letter 34), his rival for Marcus's favors—they cannot do so naively. So, whatever the relation of the letters to reality, Marcus and Fronto are playing a game, dangerous but familiar, and the letters are themselves a form of sex on paper.

This is surely a major source of the letters' reception problems in the nineteenth century. Mainstream nineteenth-century readers dealt with canonical authors by reading *around* the erotic: Catullus was bowdlerized, Petronius was read only for the comic dinner-party scene in his novel, Martial was read for the 75 percent of his epigrams that are not obscene. The rest was simply not discussed. (Meanwhile, schoolboys and shadow scholars looked for the left-out parts.) Had the letters been found earlier, might they have been more readable? In any case, the few critics after Mai who seem actually to have read the letters were very much put off by them and often remark that they are in "bad taste," without ever talking about sex. The erotic side of the letters was not something they wanted to deal with at all; they wanted rhetoric without erotics, but in the letters the two are inextricable. Indeed, Fronto uses his rhetorical skill, his passion for the mot juste, his penchant for similes and quotation, as a way to write in code—the *Phaedrus* remains a key text throughout—and Marcus follows suit.

Rhetoric

One fascinating thing about Roman culture in all periods—as also about Greek culture or rabbinic culture—is the way in which men jockey for prestige through displays of rhetoric, at all levels from school through the courtroom and the concert hall. In the second century CE, rhetorical display was so popular that the best rhetoricians had a status like that of rock stars today, particularly the Syrian Marcus Antonius Polemo (see letters 19, 20, 22) and the notorious Gallic eunuch Favorinus (on both, see Gleason 1995). Not surprisingly, all aspects of oratory were permeated with gendered meaning, from sentence structure and word choice to the studied gestures that characterized great oratory (see letters 32, 33). Students of rhetoric were particularly urged not to sound or look effeminate, and rhetorical contests were framed as competitions in masculinity (see Richlin 1996, 1997, 1999). Thus Fronto's descriptions of himself are manly (see letter 21); Marcus replies in kind; and Fronto coaches Marcus in walking the line between honest/manly and shamelessly popular/effeminate speech (see letter 20).

Pedagogy

Since power in public speaking was indispensable to any public career, all Roman citizen boys whose families could afford it sent them to study at a school of rhetoric; their practice sessions were known as *declamation*. A skilled speaker could make a career for himself not only as an advocate but also as a trainer of the young; many of these teachers came from outside Italy (especially Syria) and were Greek speakers, and some were even freed slaves. At the highest levels of society, parents would take their adolescent sons to study with the most eminent advocate possible. Marcus Tullius Cicero (106–43 BCE), the greatest Roman orator, participated in this system both as a student and as a mentor. We have little information on Fronto's education (see letters 34 and 44), but we do know that he took students himself, probably after the time he spent with Marcus and his adoptive brother, Lucius Verus (Haines 2.240–47 = *Ad amicos* 1.9, 10, 20, 25 = van den Hout, pp. 177, 184, 185–86).

In such a markedly homosocial environment, it is again not surprising to find that sexual tension was a common feature. Jokes, gossip, and anecdotes about teachers having sex with students are easy to find (see Richlin 1993, 537–38; compare Hubbard 2005 on classical Greek culture). One of the most substantial stories comes from the *Satyricon,* Petronius's comic novel (85–86): the poet Eumolpus tells about how, when he was a civil servant in the Near East, at Pergamum, he became tutor to a teenage boy, whom he attempted to seduce, bribing him with gifts. At the end of the story, the roles have been reversed, and the boy now threatens Eumolpus with disclosure if he stops performing. This tale has a lot to say about sexual norms, what was respectable, what parents might have been expected to think about such a relationship, the circumstances in which it might take place, and the risk taken by the participants.

Sexuality, of course, plays a major role in philosophical training, as seen in the works of Plato, particularly the *Phaedrus* and the *Symposium.* The love of women fades from view almost completely, and the philosopher's involvement with the beauty of young men prefigures his knowledge of the beauty of truth. The *Phaedrus,* which begins with heavy flirting between Socrates and Phaedrus, continues with two speeches on boys and their lovers and "nonlovers," one of which forms the model for letter 2 in this collection. The *Phaedrus* goes on with two major sections, one on love and the other on rhetoric, a combination that is central to the intellectual world of Marcus and Fronto. But it is the section on love that most readers remember, with its image of the soul as a winged charioteer with a team of winged horses, one of which, the bad, uncontrollable horse, keeps lusting after boys. More than two thousand years later, John Addington Symonds would reproach Benjamin Jowett for teaching Oxford students to read the *Phaedrus* while insisting it was not about sex (see Dowling 1994, 89, 128–30); as always with Plato, a text about sex is also about something else but is still a text about sex.

Much less familiar to modern readers is the position of the early Stoic philosophers on sexuality. Zeno (335–263 BCE) and his successor, Chrysippus (280–207 BCE), argued that sex between human beings who have learned the proper principles of respect and true friendship is a good thing, and that the ideal society would be one in which sex was enjoyed freely, without propertarian bonds of marriage. In particular, the young person just turning toward philosophy, the *prokoptôn,* should be trained by his mentor first through a sexual relationship, which should grow into an understanding of philosophy (see Gaca 2003, 59–81). Although the Stoic tenets are unisex, Zeno was known in ancient histories of philosophy as someone interested only in boys, not in women at all, and by the second century CE the Stoics were commonly joked about as interested, not just in boys, but in boys past the usual age limits for pederasty. Stoics of the Roman empire like Seneca and Plutarch turned away from these norms toward an emphasis on marriage (see Gaca 2003, 82–93), but we know Marcus was reading early Stoic work (letter 42; but see n. 5).

This, then, is the uneasy setting for the relationship between Marcus and Fronto. On the one hand, a philosophical and pedagogical ideal prescribes that they be at least emotionally close; on the other, Roman traditions of mentorship and the language of rhetorical theory caution against any hint of playing the feminine role. Under law, a man charged with seducing an adolescent male citizen could be sued by the boy's family or possibly prosecuted under the adultery laws, which were criminal; by the early third century, and perhaps earlier, the penalty for a completed seduction was death, for an attempted one deportation to an island (see Richlin 1993, 562–66). Gossip was always only too ready to impute sexual misconduct to a teacher-student relationship, as in the *Invective against Cicero,* where the gleefully outspoken attacker says: "Haven't you lived so from your boyhood that you thought nothing sinful for your body that anybody wanted to do? Isn't it a fact that you studied up that excessive eloquence of yours from Marcus Piso at the cost of your chastity?" (pseudo-Sallust *Against Cicero* 2). And Marcus Aurelius was not just any student—this was the future emperor. Who was Fronto, really? An outsider. If there were to be a pederastic relationship between Fronto and his imperial charge, it would have to be careful and secret; letters would be extremely risky; they would have to follow a strict code of plausible deniability. Arguably, that is exactly what we have in the Marcus-Fronto letters.

Marriage

Even the most thoroughgoing fans of pederasty among the ancient philosophers agreed that a healthy state depended on the continued production of citizens; Plato and Zeno both, even in their most radical utopias, require mating between men and women for the purpose of bearing children and (after citizens' begetting days are over) allow it just for fun (see Gaca 2003). Many pederastic texts exist in a milieu that takes the marriage of adult males for granted, and wives are said in jokes to be jealous of their husband's suspected sex partners, boys or women indifferently.

Thus it is perfectly normal that Fronto might have a romantic interest in Marcus while enjoying what seems to have been a happy marriage; his wife's name was Cratia. He does not say much about her, but she travels about independently of him, and the letters speak of her visits to Marcus's mother, Domitia Lucilla, and to Marcus, whom Domitia Lucilla seems to have lived with pretty continually, even as he moved from imperial villa to villa. No letters to Cratia are extant or even mentioned. She may have been Greek by birth, judging from her name. Cratia and Fronto have only one child, named Cratia after her mother; we hear in a gut-wrenching later letter from Fronto to Marcus that he has had six children but was never the parent of more than one child at a time (Haines 2.222–23 = *De nepote amisso* 2 = van den Hout, pp. 235–39). Cratia, in other words, gave birth to six children, five of whom died in infancy before the next one was born.

Marcus's position was more unusual. First of all, he is the only Roman male I can think of whose relationship with his mother is so closely detailed. Domitia Lucilla is mentioned at the end of almost every letter between Marcus and Fronto before 145 CE—at least scholars assume that she is the one meant in the recurring sign-offs: "My Lady says hello"; "Say hello to your Lady." In one memorable letter, Domitia Lucilla even comes in and has a sort of bedside chat with Marcus, all about their love for, respectively, Cratia and Fronto (see letter 39). Fronto also indicates that he is in the habit of writing to her regularly (see letter 21, a letter written in Greek, probably in tribute to her erudition, although somewhat ambivalent in tone); another Greek letter to her is extant, conveying birthday wishes (Haines 1.146–51 = *Epist. Graec.* 2 = van den Hout, pp. 32–33). In letter 15, Fronto seems to be hinting that he is worried she may be reading Marcus's effusive letters—or maybe not.

Another person seems to turn into the "Lady" in question after 145 CE: Marcus's new wife, Faustina, in whom Marcus shows surprisingly little interest. She is not mentioned before the marriage and remains a cipher in the letters—less of a presence than Marcus's mother; she is known to history principally through the insinuations of her sexual promiscuity in the *Historia Augusta,* which inspired Swinburne's poem "Faustine." Pater in *Marius the Epicurean* made her very much the wronged innocent, although something of a femme fatale, basing this on the *Historia Augusta*'s reports of Marcus's affectionate tolerance of her. She bore Marcus twelve children between 147 and 166 CE, which was quite unusual for an upper-class Roman woman and perhaps shows how seriously Marcus took Zeno. Only one of the boys lived past childhood: Commodus.

It would certainly have been normative for an *erômenos* to end that role on leaving adolescence; love poetry specifies that the acquisition of adult physical characteristics ends the boy's attractiveness (see Richlin 1992, 35, 42). Ancient texts do not discuss the young man's abrupt transition from sex object to subject, which must have been difficult; there are some stories about older adolescents as attractive to women as well as to men (see Konstan 2002; Walters 1993). The cryptic word *exoletus* (grown up, overblown, [over]ripe), used of male prostitutes or sex slaves, may have something to do with the problem—but, as usual, from the point of view of the consumer rather than the consumed. In any case, soon after his marriage Marcus had to cope with the birth of his first child and the assumption of a great many more political duties; van den Hout (1999, 186) suggests that the concomitant increase in authority may lie behind his rejection of rhetoric for his beloved philosophy. But the post-145 letters certainly give no indication that Faustina has become the focus of Marcus's devotion as Fronto had been, although many of his letters (now short) deal with his children.

Kissing

One thing the letters are not is sexually explicit. The main physical expression that comes up is kissing, and the reader may well wonder how sexual this kissing is. It was certainly a social convention in this period for men to greet one another with a kiss, and in many jokes of the comic poet Martial, who wrote about forty years before Marcus and Fronto, this is a kiss on the lips. As with the convention of flowery language, the reader can look at letters Fronto wrote to other friends to see whether there is a difference between, on the one hand, Marcus's terms of endearment and the way Marcus and Fronto talk about kisses and, on the other, how Fronto writes to other people. I would argue that, yes, there is quite a difference.

Illness and the Body

Many readers of the whole letter collection have commented on Marcus and Fronto's obsession with their health. Often they tell us more than we really want to know about their symptoms. Both Michel Foucault (1988, 99–144) and Judith Perkins (1995, 7–8, 142–72), writing on asceticism in the second century CE, have talked about a concern with bodily health as typical of this period. However, I would say that the concern with health in the letters of 139–45 is different from what it comes to be later. Here, Fronto's aches and pains give Marcus an excuse to talk about his body, and Marcus's colds are an excuse for both of them to fuss a little; they indulge in mutual coddling. Later, Fronto's ill health turns into an expression of self-pity, while Marcus's turns into a substitute for what came before. Similarly thought-provoking is the letters' obsession with sleep, wakefulness, and dreams, along with Marcus's habit of writing in bed (see letter 4).

Mechanics of Letter Writing and Publication

Ancient books were not published in the modern sense; the number of copies of each text would be small, and books were expensive, a luxury item (see Harris 1989, 224–25). (Indeed, this continued to be true well into the nineteenth century, especially so for books in Latin and Greek; antiquity was not knowable for most people before the broadening of education not much more than a hundred years ago.) Works were copied by hand onto rolls of papyrus. Ancient letter collections were divided by their editors into "books," that is, long sections, usually distinguished by addressee. Thus we have Cicero's letters to his best friend, Atticus (a collection divided into sixteen books), and then, also in sixteen books, his letters to his *familiares* (usually translated "friends"), among which are his letters to his wife, Terentia (bk. 14, only twenty-one letters), and his letters to his freed slave, Tiro (bk. 16, twenty-seven letters), along with smaller collections addressed to his brother Quintus and to Marcus Brutus. Modern editors have often wanted to reshuffle Cicero's letters and put them in chronological order; Mary Beard (2002) has suggested that through this process we may be losing a sense of the letter book as a literary creation. The Fronto letters in van den Hout's 1988 edition are divided into fourteen books—five books to Marcus as Caesar (Marcus's name as designated successor to the empire); four to the emperor Antoninus (that is, to Marcus as emperor); two to the emperor Verus (Marcus's adoptive brother); one to Antoninus Pius; and two to Fronto's friends—plus assorted essays. The notes to this translation will sometimes comment on the placement of a letter within the original letter collection, but I have chosen to follow a chronological arrangement.

However, it must be confessed that, unlike Cicero's, these letters carry no dates of any kind; it would be normal to give at least the day of the month, while the year could be indicated by referring to the consuls whose names marked the year (at this point in the empire there would be several sets of consuls each year; only the first set got the year named after them). The only letters that can be dated with any degree of certainty are those that give Marcus's age and those to and from Fronto as consul, since the year of his consulship is known: 143 CE. The order of the present translation is derived from consideration of scholarly opinion, of any internal evidence, and, in what I regret to say is a circular argument, of the level of emotion expressed. In 145 Marcus got married; the following year he told Fronto pretty explicitly that he was no longer interested in rhetoric (see letter 42); the relationship deteriorated drastically after that point. Edward Champlin (1974), Fronto's biographer, has classified many of the Marcus-Fronto letters as only roughly datable; I think it is reasonable to guess that an effusive letter carrying no other datable mark was written before 145. For the most part, I follow Haines and (a bit less so) van den Hout in their sense of when the letters come; together, they spent more time with Marcus and Fronto than almost anyone but Hauler and Naber and Mai.

Unlike the published letters of, say, Virginia Woolf, the Marcus-Fronto letters do not come to you at a single remove. I wish I could sit down, open a box, and take from it the actual letters from the hand of Fronto, but that chance is long gone. It was not even so common for Romans to write their letters themselves; upper-class Romans had slaves to take dictation, so we would not ordinarily hope to see our protagonists preserved in ink. One of the key features of the Marcus-Fronto letters, however, is the string of reminders by each to each that he is writing with his own hand (letters 9, 12, 18, 22, 32, 33; letters 40 and 41 comment on a lapse in their practice). This points to what might be considered a strain of fetishism in the collection, as the paper comes to stand in for the absent person himself—a familiar trope in letter writing (see Altman 1982; Stewart 1984). Countless love songs in our own culture depend on the tie between letter writing and longing, and I recommend reading these letters while listening to Toussaint McCall singing "Nothing Takes the Place of You." Plato himself says that desire must be for what one has not (*Symposium* 200a).

Letters at this time might be written on *tabellae,* writing tablets made of thin sheets of wood coated with wax on which the words were incised with a stylus, or on a papyrus scroll (more expensive) using a reed pen or calamus (and the word *calamus* must resonate with fans of Walt Whitman). Marcus and Fronto tend to indicate that they are using papyrus. Either way, the letter would often be sealed with wax and the wax marked with the print of the writer's signet; in one letter, Fronto tells Marcus that he has not only sealed the letter but also sewed up its edges. Letters were delivered by slaves who acted as messengers (see letters 15, 40) and, of course, could also be delivered by a friend (see letter 20, where the carrier is Marcus's friend Victorinus, whose curiosity has caused Fronto to sew up his letter). It seems likely that Fronto kept copies of his own letters (see his letter to Marcus as emperor where he talks about a much earlier letter, Haines 2.38–39 = *Ant. imp.* 1.2 = van den Hout, p. 88, lines 14–15) rather than that someone later managed to get access to some royal archive to retrieve them, but this is just a guess. The process of assembly of ancient letter books before Fronto is attested by few— but tantalizing—clues (on Cicero and Pliny, see Beard 2002, 116–24).

Indeed, the question of how and why these letters came to be preserved and copied over is one of the mysteries surrounding them. Although some of the material in the letter book seems to have been written for show, much of it does not, and Fronto probably did not intend to publish the collection himself (see Champlin 1980, 3). Fronto's long-winded contemporary and fan, Aulus Gellius, never mentions the letters. Perhaps they were kept in the family out of pride in Fronto's reputation and in his friendship with emperors, and were published, in a limited way, by a much later descendant who wanted to boost his own claim to aristocracy (see Champlin 1974, 156–57; Zetzel 2000). The copy of the letters that Mai found under the supervening text in the palimpsest was probably made in the late fifth century CE (see Zetzel 1980); from the time of Fronto's death (around 166 CE) to the late seventh century, when this copy was erased for reuse, very few instances of clear citations of the letters are known—and none of those that are known are dated earlier than the early fourth century CE (see van den Hout 1988, xiv–xv, 267–70; compare the discussion above of Marcus's *Meditations,* also uncited before this period).

Of this silence and loss, I can here comment further only that the late second century was an inauspicious time to come on the literary scene; the third century was to be a time of political chaos, and, by 225 CE, Latin literary production at Rome seems to have ground to a halt, or else most of it just got lost. (Not that there wasn't action elsewhere.) The Roman intelligentsia pops into sight again in the late third century—and may well have been there all along—but its means of circulating texts seem to have shrunk or changed. It was an obscure writer of the late third century, Nemesianus, who produced the last extant pederastic poetry. The fourth-century readers who quote from Fronto's letters—Nazarius, Charisius, and possibly Symmachus and Servius—are precisely the sort of upper-class, highly educated traditionalists who would have appreciated them. The fifth-century Gallo-Roman poet and letter writer Sidonius Apollinaris thinks highly of Fronto and brings him up repeatedly, but only as an orator, never as a role model; there is no clear sign that he knew the letters. Sidonius was also a bishop, with conflicting feelings about his taste for classical literature, and his voluminous writings carefully avoid any mention of pederasty. More and more, the texts that would be preserved are Christian or of obvious use to Christians, which the Marcus-Fronto letters are not.

ON THE LATIN TEXT

The translation here makes use of Haines's 1919–20 Loeb edition, which is often good, as well as van den Hout's 1988 Teubner. Readers who want to follow the Latin and Greek can thus use Haines fairly conveniently, and, unlike the Teubner, the Loeb should be available pretty widely and is still in print. The notes mark variant manuscript readings that are of any substantive interest, but marking all variants would have made the notes much too long, as expert readers, I hope, will understand. Just think about what happened to Hauler before you get too excited about fixing this text.

One convention of classical editing needs explanation here: where the manuscript is illegible but I am accepting an editor's guess at some missing words, the words in question are enclosed in angle brackets < >, as they are in the Latin or Greek text.

NOTES ON TRANSLATION

The translations in this volume are word for word, or close to it. So are Haines's Loeb translations, and I did not immediately see any need for a new version. But Haines, though faithful to the Latin and clever in devising pun for pun, alliteration for alliteration, writes in a style that might be described as *Pateresque*. I would guess that he was a follower of Pater—certainly he quotes him (see Haines 1919–20, 1:xxii, xxxvii)—except that Pater was the most influential stylist of his day and might well have left his mark on Haines at some remove. In any case, a reader who has not already developed a taste for Pater's dainty Victorian pedantry might well not get a good sense of the Latin from Haines's translation; and, although the style of the letters, especially Fronto's, is arguably to Latin what Pater's was to English, I wanted the letters to be readable now.

So where Marcus uses a strong image, so do I, and where Marcus makes a double entendre, so do I, and where Marcus uses slang, I use current slang and not Victorian slang. I also use contractions, which Latin makes much less use of than does English; in close reading of the letters, again especially Marcus's, it became clear to me that uncontracted English is much more formal than their Latin, so most instances of *is not* became *isn't,* and so on. Both Marcus and Fronto spent a lot of time reading Roman comedy, which is full of contractions, double entendres, and slang (although it would have been as dated by Marcus and Fronto's day as Elizabethan slang is today); it has left clear traces in their style. For that matter, and counter to the opinion of most readers since 1815, let me observe that the letters are often and intentionally funny—more Marcus than Fronto, who, after all, was playing a much riskier game. But the one speech of Fronto's excerpted by Marcus is funny in the manner of Cicero's *Pro Caelio*—a performance piece for the courtroom (see letter 32).

Marcus and Fronto also pepper their letters with snippets of Greek, and I've turned these into snippets of French where I could. Three letters were originally entirely in Greek: letter 2, a literary pastiche, I put into quasi-eighteenth-century English; letters 21 and 34 are just in English, although French would give a better sense of the letters' bilingualism and tone. Also, where possible, I have translated quotations from early Latin authors as quotations from Shakespeare, a practice that, odd as these may sound, gives a much better feel for the texture of the letters than a literal translation can.

Some words were hard to translate:

1. Latin is fortunate in having the word *iste,* a demonstrative adjective like *this* or *that* that also conveys distaste, contempt, or a teasing association between something the writer dislikes and the person he is addressing: "that hat of yours"; "that author you like." When *iste* comes up—and both Marcus and Fronto use it constantly—I have tried to get the tone just by using *that,* but, where I couldn't, the reader will see, for example, *that damn, those stupid, that annoying.*

2. Marcus often addresses Fronto as *magister,* which I have translated throughout as *teacher.* It does mean "teacher," and that is what Marcus means by it, but *magister* comes from the Latin *magis,* "more," and has a wide range of other meanings—head priest, ship captain, chief officer, commander, local official, manager, emcee, shepherd, expert. The English word *master* is derived from it, and *master* in the English sense "teacher" or "mentor" would be the best translation for it, but that sense is growing dim, while the sense "slave owner" has grown strong. And one thing *magister* does not mean in Latin is "slave owner." So Marcus's *magister* conveys a sometimes ironic, sometimes teasing sense of addressing a superior—which, of course, was a problem in the relationship between prince and teacher, Roman aristocrat and provincial, eighteen and forty-four.

On the other hand, Fronto often addresses Marcus as *dominus,* the correct title for addressing the emperor (both Marcus and Fronto use it for Antoninus Pius), but *dominus* does also mean "slave owner." It is here translated as *Lord* throughout.

It is worth noting that Fronto usually calls Marcus either *dominus* or *Caesar,* almost never *Marcus,* while Marcus often calls him *Fronto*—and never just *Marcus,* which was Fronto's first name, too.

3. There are three words for "kiss" in Latin—*basium, osculum,* and *savium.* They are famously differentiated by the antiquarian scholar Servius in the fourth century CE: *basium* is the kiss you give your wife, *osculum* is the kiss you give your children, and *savium* (associated with *voluptas,* "pleasure") is the kiss you give a whore (*Commentary on the "Aeneid,"* at line 1.256). In the first century BCE love poet Catullus, of whose work there are many echoes in the letters, *savium* seems to mean "French kiss"; this is very explicitly so in the poem quoted by Fronto's contemporary Aulus Gellius that appears here in n. 17, letter 44. *Basium* does not appear in the Marcus-Fronto letters, and *savium* makes a startling appearance in some places where the one kissed definitely does not seem to be eroticized ("your mother" [letter 20]; "my daughter" [letter 46]); could this be a joke? Meanwhile, *osculum* here seems to denote some definitely erotic kisses, as it certainly does in Catullus. I have had to deal with this in the notes.

4. Colloquial Latin likes to put diminutive endings on nouns (*-ulus, -olus, -unculus, -ellus*); they are all over Plautus, Cicero's letters, and Petronius. Marcus in particular loves diminutives, and in his letters I have translated many of them using the word *tiny;* his use of diminutives verges, I think, on the sarcastic or facetious.

P.S.

The pleasure of reading letters is always voyeuristic, snoopy—irresistible, with its illusion of being there, of knowing the past and the other at first hand. Especially in a long-term correspondence between two people, like the Marcus-Fronto letters, the spying reader sees the building of an intimate world, in which shared experiences and readings, and the unreeling spool of the letters themselves, spawn code words, metonyms for wholes at which the tantalized reader can only guess. After all, what is a code for but to exclude "them" and include "us"? Fronto says as much—"Let people doubt, talk, argue, guess, quest after the origin of our love, just like the sources of the Nile" (letter 15)—perhaps echoing Catullus to Lesbia. The nameless, hypothetical compiler removed some pieces and perhaps altered others; time tripled his efforts; fashion buried it all in a corner. Now you hold Marcus and Fronto in your hands, and with the breath of each turn of the page they begin to breathe again. Go on—take a look.

SUGGESTIONS FOR FURTHER READING

Ancient Writers

Along with Haines's Loeb translation of Fronto's complete letter collection into English (1919–20), the letters have been translated into Italian by Felicità Portalupi (1974) and into French by Pascale Fleury and Ségolène Demougin (2003), who, however, chose to print only letters by Fronto himself.

The Penguin translations of the letters of Cicero and the younger Pliny are good and widely available, although these letters are not erotic; there are a few expressions of love in Cicero's letters to his wife, more in those to his freed slave Tiro (see esp. *Letters to His Friends* 16.27, Quintus Cicero to Tiro), and some in Pliny's letters to his wife. Amatory expressions in Cicero's correspondence with his younger male friends take some finding; see *Letters to His Friends* 7.15.1 (to Trebatius); 8.3.1 (Caelius to Cicero); 15.21.1 (to Trebonius); 9.14.4 (to Dolabella). See Trapp 2003 for a good overview of ancient letter writing with examples of various types, from real to fictional. Readers interested in love letters in particular should look at Costa 2001 and might well want a more in-depth look at the *Erotic Epistles* of Philostratus, available in the Benner and Fobes (1949) translation— these are literary letters, though (see Rosenmeyer 2001, esp. 322–38). Readers interested in letters written by ordinary people can find an archaeological miracle—a collection from a remote military out-post in northern Britain in the early second century CE—in Bow-man 1994, and a great many papyrus letters from Greco-Roman Egypt translated in Hunt and Edgar 1932 (268–395), in Rowland-son 1998, and in Bagnall and Cribiore 2005, although, as Dominic Montserrat explains (1996, 5–13), there's nothing much in the way of love letters known on papyrus. For a sense of the world in which Marcus and Fronto lived, ancient novels are also illuminating, though highly romanticized; the Greek novels are collected in Reardon 1989, and Petronius's *Satyricon* is available in several good translations, as is Apuleius's *Metamorphoses* (also titled *The Golden Ass*). Sarah Ruden's *Satyricon* translation (2000) includes excellent background information. The *Historia Augusta* is translated in both the Pen-guin and Loeb series (Birley 1976; Magie 1921).

For those interested in letter 2 and Plato's *Phaedrus,* Nehamas and Woodruff (1995) provide not only a translation of the *Phaedrus* but also a good introduction and notes.

Textual Transmission

On the question of how ancient texts came down to us, *Scribes and Scholars* (Reynolds and Wilson 1974) provides a highly reader-friendly and enjoyable introduction.

History of the Period

The only biography of Fronto available in English is Champlin 1980, which is especially good on Fronto's African background and on the players in his political and literary life. Books on Marcus Aurelius, on the other hand, are numerous; for an accessible biography, see Birley 1987. Maud Gleason's *Making Men* (1995) provides a lively in-troduction to the great rhetoricians of the period; Leofranc Holford-Strevens's *Aulus Gellius* (1988), while more technical, is full of stories about the people who can be glimpsed at the edges of the Marcus-Fronto letters and the intellectual milieu in which Fronto moved.

Thomas Hubbard's comprehensive reader of primary sources on same-sex eroticism (2003) will take the reader well into the context of the Marcus-Fronto letters. Larmour, Miller, and Platter (1998) provide a range of critiques and corrections of Michel Foucault's work on ancient sexuality, which is not entirely reliable (Foucault 1988 covers this period). Bernadette Brooten's *Love between Women* (1996) is the main source on same-sex eroticism between women in antiquity and deals with Greek, Roman, Egyptian, Hebrew, and Christian material. Kathy Gaca (2003) gives the most thorough and accurate overview of attitudes toward sexuality in ancient philosophy and early Christianity. For those interested in the relationship between Marcus and Fronto as a friendship, David Konstan (1997) provides a good overview of the concept of friendship throughout antiquity.

K. J. Dover's *Greek Homosexuality* (1978) concentrates on classical Athens; major contributions to this area, mostly focusing on sex between males, include Davidson 1997, 2001; Halperin 1990; and Winkler 1990. On homoerotic and homophobic vocabulary in Aristophanes, which is considered by Dover but not by Foucault, see Henderson 1991; Aristophanes is important for a sense of the invective tradition.

On Roman sexuality, see Hallett and Skinner 1997 and Richlin 1992. For male same-sex eroticism, see Richlin 1993, Walters 1993, Williams 1999, and, in art, Clarke 1998.

Marilyn Skinner (2005) provides a good basic overview of Greek and Roman sex/gender systems from Homer to Hadrian (21–191 Greek, 192–282 Roman): clearly written, well illustrated, accessible.

The Victorian Audience

Suzanne Marchand's *Down from Olympus* (1996) gives a richly detailed, page-turning history of the development of classical scholarship in nineteenth-century Germany and is a must for anyone who wants to understand our own attitudes toward Greece and Rome. Same-sex male eroticism in Victorian England has been well documented by Joseph Bristow (1995) and Linda Dowling (1994); for a detailed look at some correspondence between men of less-exalted social status, see Hansen 1992. Walter Pater's novel *Marius the Epicurean* (1885) is a hard read but does feature Marcus and Fronto as characters. It gives a good sense of the moral issues facing Pater and his circle, on which see further Adams 1995; Billie Inman's essay (1991) on the love letters between Pater and William Money Hardinge, a classic example of historical detective work, makes those issues much clearer. Lillian Faderman (1998) provides an overview of women's same-sex eroticism and sentimental friendships in the West from the sixteenth century to the twentieth; Eve Sedgwick (1992) focuses on men's relationships in English literature. Readers of the Marcus-Fronto letters might also enjoy Yopie Prins's *Victorian Sappho* (1990). Alan Bray (2003) deals with sworn same-sex friendship from the eleventh century to the nineteenth and includes an afterword (307–23) that explains the political implications of the study of friendship for historians of the family.

Letter Writing

Janet Altman's *Epistolarity* (1982) provides a clear theoretical introduction to letters in literature; Susan Stewart's *On Longing* (1984) is good for thinking about why people write and keep letters.

TRANSLATIONS, QUOTATIONS, AND CITATIONS OF ANCIENT SOURCES

All translations of Latin and Greek in this book are my own unless otherwise noted.

The lack of a standard citation format for the Fronto letters makes references cumbersome; see the concordance at the end of this volume for an explanation of reference style herein. Within the text I have followed the format used in the concordance, slightly condensed.

The experience of preparing this book for the press has made me realize how inaccessible classical texts still are to the average reader. Some are still not translated, or the translation cannot be easily found; many translations do not follow the original text exactly; and exact reference to classical texts is made through a system that is unfamiliar to most people and varies from genre to genre and even author to author. For example, a reference to Plautus *Rudens* 349 here (n. 15, letter 45) means "line 349 of Plautus's play *Rudens*," but any given translation of this play may or may not translate line for line, or even indicate line numbers. Nor is there any standard translation of the titles of ancient works. I must admit, then, that many of the references to classical texts in the notes pose problems for most readers and will be of use mainly to classical scholars. I have tried to provide references to accessible translations of the more obscure works I thought would be of interest to readers of this book. But readers should be aware that references to classical texts are usually not by page number but by line number (for poetry) or book and section number (prose). Readers may also be puzzled by Latin and Greek words that appear in the notes with different endings (e.g., *libellos, libellus*). These are not misprints; words in Latin and Greek show their grammatical use by changing their endings.

LETTERS

Letter 1

MARCUS TO FRONTO, ? DECEMBER, 139 CE

Hi,[1] my very best teacher,

If you get some sleep after the all-nighters[2] you've been moaning about, please write and tell me; and please, first of all, take care of your health. Then—that bridge you keep threatening to burn— get rid of the matches and put them away[3] somewhere, and don't you let go of your plans to go to court.[4] Or, if you do, everybody else should shut their mouth too.

You say you've hammered together something or other in Greek[5] that pleases you like few things you've written. Aren't you the one who was just setting me straight[6] about "to what end[7] was I writing in Greek"? So now I really have to write something in Greek more than ever. Want to know why? I want to take a risk and see if what I didn't learn will fall in line for me more easily, because what I did learn has deserted me. But if you loved me, you would have sent me this brand-new thing you say you like. Still, I'm reading you here whether you want me to or not, and really that's the one thing I live and survive by.

Gory homework[8] you sent me! I haven't read the passage from Coelius[9] you sent yet, and I won't read it before I've tracked down the ideas for myself. But the Caesar speech[10] holds me down in its crooked claws. I finally understand now how much work it is to turn three or four lines out on my lathe[11] and write a thing day after day.

Good-bye, breath of my life. Should I not burn with love of you when you've written this to me? What should I do? I can't stop. Funny how at this same place and at this same time last year it was my lot in life to burn up with longing for my mother. This year it's you—you set this same longing alight in me. My Lady says hello.

Notes

1. Hi: This is an unusual way to begin a letter; Marcus's letters are the first in Latin to use this style regularly, and it is found only in his early letters. Fronto occasionally picks it up from him, e.g., in a quick follow-up to letter 9 (see Haines 1.66–67 = *M. Caes.* 3.4 = van den Hout, p. 38).

2. all-nighters: Marcus uses the word *vigilias,* which means "wakefulness" but has a range of specific connotations: insomnia; a soldier's alert night watch; burning the midnight oil; all-night orgies or ecstatic rituals. The theme of sleep, wakefulness, and dreams recurs throughout the letters, with all these connotations in circulation.

3. bridge . . . away: Marcus uses the image of the "ax of Tenedos," a proverbial expression for cutting off discussion. It is based on the myth of Tenes, who, when approached by his father, who had tried to kill him, cut the mooring rope of his father's boat with an ax.

4. go to court: Fronto was an eminent litigator.

5. something or other in Greek: The reference here is probably to the essay incorporated in letter 2, along with the two Greek letters mentioned there (on which see n. 3, letter 2).

6. setting me straight: Lat. *concastigabas,* "reproving," lit. "making me *castus* [chaste]."

7. to what end: Lat. *quorsum.* This is a favorite word of Fronto's (see, e.g., letters 15, 20); Marcus is here parodying him.

8. homework: Lat. *materiam,* i.e., a set theme to declaim on.

9. Coelius: The Roman historian Lucius Coelius Antipater (second century BCE), who wrote a history of the Second Punic War (which would naturally be gory). Fronto seems to have sent Marcus a set theme with instructions to declaim on it after the style of Coelius; Marcus wants to do it for himself before looking at the model.

10. the Caesar speech: Lat. *Caesaris oratio,* lit. "speech of Caesar." This phrase has sometimes been taken to refer to a putative speech of thanks that Marcus was to give for one of his official appointments, the most likely of which would date this letter to the second half of 139 CE, possibly to December. The word "Caesar" here would then point to Marcus's status as heir to the empire and beneficiary of privileges; Haines translates "my Caesar-speech." The end of the letter perhaps implies that Fronto has become Marcus's teacher within the past twelve months,

so a date between mid-139 and mid-140 seems likely in any case. However, I doubt that the phrase *Caesaris oratio* can mean "the speech I am to give in my capacity as Caesar"; in a paragraph devoted to homework, it seems more naturally to refer to a common sort of rhetorical exercise (see n. 8 above) in which the student would be assigned to write a speech in the persona and style of a famous man, the "Caesar" here probably being Julius. The historian Sallust is a favorite author of Fronto's (see n. 6, letter 7) and appears in other assignments; possibly the model here is the speech Sallust puts in Julius Caesar's mouth in his *Catiline's Conspiracy* (51). Letter 2 constitutes a similar exercise carried out by Fronto himself: a version of a speech put in the orator Lysias's mouth by Plato. See van den Hout 1999, 107–8, 112, 229, for a wide range of opinions on the meaning of this phrase and on the date of the letter; Champlin 1974, 143. Possibly this is a joke in which Marcus speaks of himself in the third person as if being Caesar and speaking as Caesar were *like* the sort of rhetorical impersonation he did as homework. See n. 6, letter 3, for Fronto's use of the phrase *eloquentiam Caesaris* (Caesar's rhetoric) in a letter to Marcus, meaning both "the rhetoric of someone who is Caesar" and "your rhetoric."

11. turn . . . lathe: This simile, familiar in Latin, goes back to Plato's *Phaedrus* 234e, in Socrates' evaluation of the *erôtikos logos* of Lysias (see n. 1, letter 2). If Marcus's simile here is an indication that he knew the *Phaedrus* well, as is likely (see Trapp 1990), that would make Fronto's choice in letter 2 even more shrewd.

Letter 2

<Discourse on Love>[1]

O dear Boy,[2] I send you this Epistle, the third upon the same Topick: the first by way of *Lysias* the Son of *Cephalus,* the second by way of *Plato* the Philosopher, and the third[3] by way of this foreign Man, whose Speech is little short of barbarick,[4] but whose Sentiment is not altogether unintelligible, as I believe. I now write touching on nothing written hitherto, lest you should slight this Discourse as discursive.[5] If it shall seem to you that this Epistle[6] is longer than those hitherto sent by way of *Lysias* and *Plato,* let the Fact that I lack not for Reasons be a Token to you that my Claims are rational. Do you apply your Wits, to know if there be not Method in my Madness.[7]

You seem likely,[8] dear Boy, to want to understand, before the compleat Discourse begins, why, pray, I who am not in love strive so eagerly to gain the same Things that Lovers do. So will I tell you first how that may be. By Zeus, that Fellow who is so very a Suitor[9] was not born with a sharper Pair of Eyes than I who am no Lover, yet I in fact am sensible of your Beauty no less than the rest; I might say, more acutely so than your Suitor. As happens, we see, the same to Men in Fevers[10] as to Men who have stripp'd for Exercise[11] at Wrestling, the same Event follows from Causes not the same. For both feel the Pains of Thirst—the one from his Malady, the other from his naked Exertions; and <it has befallen> me[12] as well to suffer some such <Malady on account of Love . . .> [two pages lost]

But me you approach not at your Peril, nor at the Cost of any Harm will you keep Company with me; nay, 'twill do you every Good. Indeed, Beauties[13] are help'd and benefitted more by those who love them not, as green Shoots are help'd by the Waters. For Springs and Rivers love not green Shoots, yet in their going near and their flowing past do they make them to flower and to bloom. Money giv'n by me you may rightly call a Gift—the Money he gives you, a Fee.[14] And the Children of the Prophets[15] say that, even to the Gods, sweeter are Thank-offerings[16] than Prayer-offerings, because the first are giv'n by the Fortunate toward the Preservation and Keeping of their Goods, while the second are giv'n by those who fare poorly, to ward off Evil. So much for the Advantages and Benefits[17] for you and for this Fellow.[18]

But if he is therefore worthy to gain your Comfort . . . you supported this yourself . . . for him you devis'd this Love and made Thes<salian Love-charms>[19] by your Art . . . you are in love . . . blameless . . . of someone because of his insa<tiable Desire> . . . except if you have been seen doing wrong. [This passage of around eleven lines is only partly legible in the manuscript.]

And be not ignorant that you yourself are wrong'd and defil'd[20] by no middling Sort of Defilement already, in that all the World knows it and openly talks of it, that this Man is your Suitor; before doing any thing of that Sort,[21] you bear the Name of doing it. Indeed most of your Countrymen call you his He-Sweetheart.[22] I, on the other Hand, will guard and keep your Name pure and undefil'd.[23] For my part you will be call'd a Beauty, but no He-Sweetheart. But if he use this Word as proper, because his Desire is greater, let him know that his Desire is not greater but more reckless. Flies and Musquitoes we most shoo from us and repel as they do fly at us most shamelessly and recklessly. Likewise wild Beasts do flee from Trackers with Hounds most of all, and Fowls from Sportsmen. Indeed all Creatures most avoid those who most lie up in wait for them and chase after them.

But if someone[24] suppose that Beauty is in higher Repute and more highly honour'd because of Suitors, he is entirely mistaken. Indeed you Beauties run the Risk of <failing to obtain> Belief in your Beauty from such as listen to your Lovers, while you will get a more steadfast Glory through us others. At least, if anyone who had never seen you should ask what you might be like to look at, he would believe me when I praise you, knowing that I am not in love with you. But he would not believe the other Fellow, as praising you not truthfully but erotickally. So such as are somehow maim'd in Body, somehow ugly and ill-form'd, would likely wish to have Suitors for themselves; for they would be woo'd by no-one but those coming to them out of erotick Frenzy and Compulsion.[25] But you, with Beauty like that, can glean nothing more at the Hands of a Lover; for those who are not in love with you need you no less. Suitors are useless to those who are really Beauties, no less than Flatterers[26] to those who are justly prais'd. In the Case of the Sea, Virtue and Credit, Honour and Gain and Ornament inhere in Sailors and Steersmen, Navy Captains[27] and Merchants and all Voyagers — not, by Zeus, in Dolphins, who cannot live but in the Sea; for Beauties, these Benefits inhere in us who praise and salute you gratis, not in Suitors, who would not be able to survive if depriv'd of Boy-Favourites.[28] You would find, if you look'd, that these Suitors are indeed the Cause of the greatest Dishonour; yet everyone who is right-minded must run away from Dishonour, especially young Men, whom Evil will oppress for a longer Time when it attacks at the beginning of a long Life.

Just as in Worship and Offerings, so also in Life, it is most fitting for Men commencing any of these <to look to> their good Name. . . . [most of a page missing] . . . Things <leading> to the most utter Disgrace . . . but to these honest Suitors it is allowed, if . . . five and . . . Money to Suitors . . . and indeed Lovers by Ornaments of such a Sort do not honour them, but play the Braggart and make a Shew, and as it were make a Dance of a Love, that should be a solemn Mystery.[29] Moreover, as all the World says, your Suitor does write down certain erotick Writings[30] about you, so as to entice you best by this Bait and lead you to him and grab you; yet these are but a Shame and a Reproach and a licentious[31] Cry shot out under the Sting of Lust, as wild Beasts or Cattle do roar because of Love, or snort or bellow or howl.[32] These Noises are like to the Songs of Lovers. In Truth were you to turn yourself over to your Suitor to be us'd wherever and whenever he wish'd, then, not waiting for the right and proper Time or Place or for Quiet or Privacy, but in the Manner of Beasts, at the Command of Lust, he would rush right to you and would want to have at you without any Regard for Decency.[33]

I will bring my Discourse to an End, only adding this one Thing more: that of all the Gifts and Works of the Gods, such as have come to the Use and Pleasure and Benefit of Mortals, some of these are divine altogether and everywhere—I mean Earth and Heaven, Sun and Sea—and we are born to sing of these and marvel at them, but not to be in love with them. But certain beautiful Things that are more trifling and find a less honourable Lot in Life, these Things are touch'd by Envy and erotick Love and Rivalry and Longing. And some men love Profit, others in turn love Victuals, others again love Wine.[34] Into these Ranks, into this sort of Class, is Beauty put by Lovers, with Profit and Victuals and Drink. But by us who marvel at it, though we are not in love with it, is Beauty put with Sun and Heaven, Earth and Sea; such things are stronger and higher than any sort of Love.

One Thing will I tell you more, that you in turn may say to other Boys and bear a Name for Sagacity. It seems likely that you are not unacquainted with a Story, whether from your Mother or those who have nurtur'd you,[35] that among the Flowers is one that loves the Sun[36] and suffers as Lovers do, rising up when the Sun rises, and turning itself round as the Sun travels the Sky, then drooping as the Sun sinks. But the Flower gains no more Profit from this, nor finds the Sun kinder because of its Love. Indeed it is the least well-regarded of green Shoots and Flowers, pick'd for neither the Feasts of Holidaymakers nor Garlands of the Gods or of Men. You seem likely, Boy, to want to see this Flower; but I will shew it to you myself, <if> we should take the Air together <outside> the City-Walls by the Illyssus . . . .[37]

Notes

1. <Discourse on Love>: This letter, really an essay, is written in Greek; it is probably the writing in Greek mentioned in letter 1. It is, in its form, a literary exercise: an imitation of a literary classic, in this case the speech of Lysias in Plato's *Phaedrus,* traditionally known as the *erôtikos logos,* "discourse on love." As M. B. Trapp says (1990, 141), "Few works were more firmly entrenched in the 'cultural syllabus' . . . by the second century AD than Plato's *Phaedrus.* . . . It must have been hard for [a student] to emerge from his education . . . without having been invited to study and admire this dialogue, and without having come to regard it as a proper model for imitation in his own literary products." Trapp provides an overview and catalog of such imitations in the second century CE, though he

omits Fronto's; several are erotic. The letter is here translated into quasi-eighteenth-century English to give some sense of the effect of the original (with apologies to the reader, and with reference to *Works of Plato Abridg'd* 1701, Collier 1701, Johnson 1756, and Macfait 1760). For the significance of Fronto's choice of this text, and for background on the *Phaedrus* as an intertext for the letters of Marcus and Fronto, see the volume introduction; n. 5, letter 3. The speech of Lysias is explicitly stated in the *Phaedrus* to have been "aimed at seducing a beautiful boy, but the speaker is not in love with him" (227c, trans. Nehamas and Woodruff 1995, 2).

2. O dear Boy: Gk. *Ô phile pai*, echoing the opening words of the *Phaedrus, Ô phile Phaidre;* Socrates throughout that dialogue addresses Phaedrus *ô phile pai. Pais,* "boy," is the word used in Greek erotica of the teenage boy beloved (see nn. 9 [on *erastês* and *erômenos*], 13 [on *kaloi*], and 28 [on *paidika*] below; and, on ancient sexuality generally, the volume introduction). *Phile* can mean "beloved," "dear," "friend"; Fronto's essay distinguishes between physical/erotic/sexual love (*erôs*) and friendly/nonphysical love (*philia,* although never here named as such). Yet, as in the *Phaedrus,* the speaker clearly is interested in physical love.

3. first . . . second . . . third: Marcus and Fronto habitually exchanged books, and perhaps Fronto has previously sent Marcus a copy of the *Phaedrus.* It is an odd way of saying so, however, and seems to mean that he sent the *Phaedrus* in installments (below, "those hitherto sent by way of *Lysias* and *Plato*"). It is perhaps more likely that he had previously sent two other pastiches, one following Lysias's speech more closely, one following Socrates' satiric imitation of Lysias. See n. 5, letter 1.

4. this . . . barbarick: Fronto refers to himself: in a later letter (see letter 21), he will describe himself as a "Libyan of the Libyan nomads." It is interesting to see this self-definition so early in Marcus and Fronto's relationship. This is the usual sort of self-deprecating remark made by a Greek or Roman writer wishing to call attention to the technical skill that he is about to display, and very like the kinds of things Socrates says of himself in Plato's dialogues; in the *Phaedrus,* e.g., he disclaims any skill as a rhetor while out-rhetoring Lysias.

5. I now write . . . discursive: Cf. *Phaedrus* 235d.

6. Epistle: Gk. *epestalmenôn*—as if Lysias and Plato had been writing to Marcus.

7. Reasons . . . Claims . . . Method . . . Madness: These sentences play with the related words *euloga,* "reasonable things" (lit. "good words"); *logoi,* "words"; and *legein,* "speak."

8. likely: Nehamas and Woodruff (1995, 1 n. 3) point out that, in the *Phaedrus,* Plato makes a running joke by using variations on the word *eikos,* "what is likely"—a favorite concept with rhetoricians like Lysias. It thus seems significant that Fronto sets *eoikas,* "you seem likely," as the first word in the speech proper;

eoikas recurs at the very end of the speech, in a deliberate reminiscence of this opening, as well as in various forms throughout the speech. See also letters 21 and 44, which deal with Fronto's fondness for similes (Gk. *eikones*).

9. Suitor: Gk. *erastês,* lit. "lover." *Erastês* and *erômenos,* "beloved," are used conventionally of, respectively, the pursuer and the pursued in a male-male sexual relationship in classical Athens, with implications about probable age (older/younger), beauty (less/more), and sexual position (penetrator/penetrated). (The penetrator/penetrated distinction is disputed for classical Athens [Davidson 1997, 2001; Hubbard 1998, 2003, 10–14], although not for Rome.) Both words, in Greek, are male in gender. On the Greek and Roman sex/gender systems, see the volume introduction. See also nn. 2 (on *pais, erôs,* and *philia*) and 13 (on *kaloi*).

10. Fevers: For love as a sickness (*nosos*), cf. *Phaedrus* 231d; this (conventional) image pervades the *Phaedrus*. Extended metaphors and similes like this were a typical part of every Platonic dialogue; Fronto, however, also claimed special expertise in similes (see letter 4, where he has assigned Marcus similes to write for homework, as well as letters 21 and 44). Letter 2 is peppered with them.

11. stripp'd for Exercise: Gk. *gumnasamenôn,* which includes the idea that those working out were naked. Wrestling classes were a much-noted locale for ogling the beautiful and possibly coming to grips with them (Hubbard 2005; see Plato *Charmides* 154a–d; Dover 1978, 54–55, 138; but also Persius 4.39; Martial 14.201; Strato *Greek Anthology* 12.206, 222; and n. 1, letter 35). And indeed, wrestling is often used in Latin as a figure for sexual intercourse.

12. me: One of the startling things about this speech is the number of "true confessions" moments, when the conceit of an imitation of Lysias seems to slip. Lysias never says he has experienced the *nosos* of love (see n. 10 above). But this passage is based on a hypothetical reconstruction of the damaged text.

13. Beauties: Gk. *hoi kaloi.* Haines, with uncharacteristic freedom, translates this as "beautiful youths," and this is certainly what is meant, although the Greek literally means "beautiful males." Haines (1919–20, 1:25 n. 2) remarks: "*Kalos* was the recognized tribute to the victorious boy-athlete, and is constantly so used on vases." It is true that "So-and-so (is) *kalos*" appears as a caption on many vases; these are now thought to be love gifts, used in seduction (see Dover 1978, 114–22). But Haines—who took his B.A. at Cambridge in 1880—may well have had in mind his alma mater, where attractive male undergraduates were known as "beauties" as recently as the 1970s (Simon Goldhill, personal communication).

14. Fee: This is cruder than anything in Lysias's speech; cf. *Phaedrus* 231a–b, where the exchange is treated entirely in terms of favors. Allusions to the prostitution of boys are avoided in Plato's dialogues (see Davidson 1997, 90–91). An interesting comparison with Fronto's text is Xenophon *Memorabilia* 1.6.13, another Socratic interchange. Xenophon's Socrates contrasts selling one's *hôra,* "bloom,"

to anyone who wants it with making a noble friend/*erastês,* and an analogy is drawn between sophistry and good citizenship. The implication here is quite insulting; such an accusation belongs more to forensic oratory than to philosophy (cf. Aeschines *Against Timarchus* or, more pertinently for Fronto, Cicero *Philippics* 2.44–47). For the ploy of defining words/actions, cf. *Phaedrus* 238b.

15. the Children of the Prophets: Gk. *manteôn . . . paides* "the prophet kind." For the theme of prophecy and divine possession in the *Phaedrus,* see Nehamas and Woodruff 1995, 3 n. 8, commenting on *Phaedrus* 228b.

16. Thank-offerings: For the theme of voluntary favors, cf. *Phaedrus* 231a. This theme will recur on a large scale in letter 15.

17. Advantages and Benefits: Favorite Platonic categories, appearing many times in the *Phaedrus* (see, e.g., 233a, 237d, 238e, 240a).

18. this Fellow: Gk. *kakeinôi.* Here and below, the speaker again conveys the impression, not of a hypothetical person, but of some specific man who is in love with the addressee.

19. Thes\<salian Love-charms\>: Thessaly was famous for witches in classical Greece and later; they are often said to make love charms, and this association shows up many times in Latin literature (e.g., in Apuleius's *Metamorphoses,* a novel roughly contemporary with Marcus and Fronto). Making such charms was not a nice thing to do, and it is an unusual imputation to make of a young man. Cf. *Phaedrus* 230d, where Socrates accuses Phaedrus of using a *pharmakon,* i.e., a potion, to beguile him. See also letter 33 at n. 12, where Fronto again associates Marcus with love charms.

20. defil'd: Gk. *hubrizomenos.* This was a strong word and includes "raped" in its range of meanings (for the translation, see Genesis 34).

21. of that Sort: The reference here is to sex. This periphrasis is in keeping with the speech of Lysias, regarding which Nehamas and Woodruff (1995, 7 n. 19) note "the speaker's reluctance to mention sex directly." But Fronto does not remain so reticent.

22. He-Sweetheart: Gk. *erômenos;* see n. 9. The word *He-Sweetheart* is borrowed from the Collier translation of Marcus Aurelius's *Meditations* (1701).

23. undefil'd: On gossip and the reputation of the *erômenos,* see *Phaedrus* 231e–232b, 234a; and below.

24. someone: The Greek gives an effect similar to the arch English use of *a certain someone* to mean "you."

25. Compulsion: Gk. *anagkên:* This is an important concept in the *Phaedrus,* though the word occurs only here in Fronto's version.

26. Flatterers: For this theme, see letter 15.

27. Navy Captains: Lit. "captains of triremes."

28. Boy-Favourites: Gk. *paidika.* This word is a noun formed from an adjec-

tive, *paidikos,* that simply means "of a boy"; hence *ta paidika* means "boy-related things." It came to have the sense "sweetie," "darling" (boy), like Lat. *deliciae.* But *paidika* would have had an extra overtone to a Latin speaker: the Latin verb *pedico,* which looks as if it were formed from *paidika,* means "bugger" and is quite coarse. The translation is borrowed from Collier 1701.

29. make a Dance . . . Mystery: Gk. *exorchountai.* Cf. Lucian *On Dancing* 15, where this verb is said to be common parlance for divulging the mysteries of Greek religious cult. For ecstatic dance and ritual in the *Phaedrus,* see Nehamas and Woodruff 1995, 3 n. 8.

30. Writings: Again, this is much more specific than anything in the *Phaedrus;* if these were real, none has survived.

31. licentious: Gk. *akolastos,* a key term in the *Phaedrus.*

32. wild . . . howl: This image is much stronger than anything in Lysias's speech.

33. In Truth . . . Decency: This is markedly more vivid than anything in Lysias's speech (on Lysias's use of periphrases, see n. 21 above). "Have at you" translates Gk. *bainein;* cf. Henderson 1991, 155, and his index s.v.

34. Profit . . . Victuals . . . Wine: Cf. *Phaedrus* 238b (in the speech of Socrates that follows the speech of Lysias).

35. Mother . . . you: The appearance of the addressee's mother is jarring in this Platonic context—Plato may sometimes use mothers to think with, but he has little interest in actual women. Marcus's mother, however, will be a recurring figure in the Marcus-Fronto letters. By "those who have nurtur'd you" is meant slaves, who would typically be in charge of young children in an elite Roman household and proverbially told them stories. Compare the historian Tacitus, a contemporary of Fronto's, complaining about the way upper-class children are raised by (Greek) slaves (*Dialogus* 29).

36. one that loves the Sun: Van den Hout (1999, 567) explains this as a reference to the sunflower and cites the story of Clytie in Ovid's *Metamorphoses* (4.256–70)—an abject and cross-gendered simile if so—but surely there is an underlying allusion to the story of Hyacinthus and Apollo. Note that this simile can be read two ways: above, the speaker has aligned "Beauties" with the sun as objects not to be loved (which would align Fronto with the flower); yet, especially with the advice to the boy to tell this story to the other boys, he seems to turn from the problem of love *for* boys to that of the love felt *by* boys. This would make Marcus the flower and Fronto the sun, a problem in their actual respective power positions that would recur with increasing force over time. But, as seen in letter 3, this seems to be how Marcus took letter 2. For a flower in similar danger in a similarly gender-ambiguous position, see Catullus 11.23.

37. You . . . Illyssus: The opening words of this sentence echo the opening of

the speech. The speaker's proposal to go for a walk down by the river Ilissus (the spelling in the translation comes from Macfait 1760) reprises the opening of the *Phaedrus,* where Phaedrus teases Socrates into going for a walk with him along the stream—actually, *in* the stream. The location outside the city walls and the mythic, rustic setting are key elements in the *Phaedrus* and will be recalled in letter 3, from Marcus to Fronto (see n. 5, letter 3).

Letter 3

Hi, my very best teacher,

Go ahead, as much as you like, threaten me, accuse me, with whole clumps of arguments, but you will never put off your Suitor[1]—I mean me. Nor will I proclaim it any less that I love Fronto, or will I be less in love, because you've proven, and with such strange and strong and elegant expressions, that those who love less should be helped out and lavished with more. God, no, I am dying so for love of you, and I'm not scared off by this doctrine of yours, and if you're going to be more ripe and ready for others who don't love you, I will still love you as long as I live and breathe.

But about the crowd of ideas, about the cleverness of your literary imagination,[2] about the brilliance of your imitation, I don't even want to say that you've outdone those oh so self-satisfied and teasing Atticists[3]—though I can't help but say it. It's because I love you, and I move that at least this really should be granted to lovers, that they take more pleasure in the victories of their He-Sweethearts.[4] We've won, then, we've won, I'm telling you. You don't think, do you, that [two lines missing here] discussion <can't> go on more outstandingly under a paneled ceiling than under the plane trees, inside the city limits than outside the walls, without a sweetie than with <Lais> herself sticking very close <and living next door>.[5] I can't get my lasso around[6] which thing I need to watch out for more—the doctrine *the* orator of our time pronounced about <Lysias> or what my teacher said about Plato.[7]

But this I'll personally swear to, no fear: If that Phaedrus guy of yours[8] ever really existed, if he was ever away from Socrates, Socrates didn't burn more with desire for Phaedrus than I've burned during these days—did I say days? I mean months—for the sight of you. Your letter fixed it so a person wouldn't have to be Dion to love you so much[9]—if he isn't immediately seized with love of you. Goodbye, my biggest thing under heaven, my pride and joy. It's enough for me to have had such a teacher. My lady mother says hello.

Notes

1. Suitor: *erastes* (here, uniquely, transliterated from Greek to Latin), "lover." On the Greek and Roman sex/gender systems, see the volume introduction. For the translation, see n. 9, letter 2—Marcus is responding to Fronto's letter.

2. literary imagination: Lat. *inventio,* the branch of rhetoric that dealt with making up arguments.

3. Atticists: Latin style was split into two camps, Asianists and Atticists, the former (including Cicero) favoring an ornate style, the latter a severe and terse style. In addition, during this period, in a literary movement known as the Second Sophistic, Greek stylists longed to return to the style of classical Athens, and are also called Atticists. Lucian, for example, writes in a style that imitates the Athenian style of six hundred years before him. Marcus's point here is that the ordinarily flowery Fronto has out-Atticized the Atticizers.

4. He-Sweethearts: Gk. *erômenoi,* "beloveds"; see nn. 9 and 22, letter 2.

5. plane trees . . . <and living next door>: This list of contrasts invokes the setting of Plato's *Phaedrus* (the basis of letter 2; for the setting, see n. 37, letter 2). There Socrates and Phaedrus go for a walk outside the city by the banks of the Ilissus and sit in the shade of a tall plane tree. This location, especially the plane tree, became emblematic of the *Phaedrus* and pops up in erotic and rhetorical literature from Cicero's time to Fronto's; see Trapp 1990, 143–47. The plane tree often connotes the scene of a pederastic idyll; cf. letter 19 at n. 5. See also Juvenal *Satires* 1.12 and Mayor's commentary ad loc.: Fronto's house may have had its own plane trees. The text is shaky; Lais does not belong here, and it is possible that the text originally said "Lysias himself" (see letter 2). Lais was a famous Athenian female prostitute.

6. get my lasso around: Lat. *reteiaclari,* lit. "throw a net over," as in hunting. This word (if this is actually what the text says) appears nowhere else in Latin, and Marcus is probably making it up on the spot; he was fond of hunting (see letters 36 and 38). Along with other things here that are unusual or unique (e.g., *clumps, erastes*), this slangy nonce word typifies Marcus's early style—breezy, inventive, warm, and a little fresh. As van den Hout notes (1999, 5), Marcus's letters are more colloquial than Fronto's. Fronto seems to be telling Marcus off for this habit in another brief letter (Haines 1.52–53 = *M. Caes.* 3.1 = van den Hout, p. 35): compared with speech that is *impudens atque impudica* (fresh and slutty), Marcus speaks in public using no unusual language, knowing that Caesar's rhetoric should be like the *tuba* (war trumpet) and not the *tibiae* (a reed instrument played at the theater and for dance performances, connoting indecency and sexual license, much as references to the saxophone do today).

7. orator . . . Plato: Both the orator and the teacher here must be Fronto.

8. that Phaedrus guy of yours: Lat. *iste Phaeder.* Contemporary lives of the philosophers speculated on Plato's actual love life; Diogenes Laertius, who wrote in the early third century CE but incorporates a lot of earlier material, includes Phaedrus among those rumored to have been Plato's *erômenoi* (*Lives of the Philosophers* 3.29, 31). Note that Marcus here throughout casts himself as *erastês* and Fronto as *erômenos,* himself as Socrates and Fronto as Phaedrus, a saucy switch on their respective ages. The question of who holds power plagues the whole relationship (see the end of letter 2 and the accompanying n. 36).

9. Your . . . much: This section of the sentence is based on a barely legible line in the manuscript and fits only bumpily with the rest of the sentence. Dion was a young Syracusan nobleman when he met Plato, whose fan he became and whom he involved in Sicilian politics. He is also one of those listed by Diogenes Laertius as among Plato's *erômenoi* (*Lives of the Philosophers* 3.29–30); see n. 8 above.

Letter 4

To my teacher,

When you rest and when you do what's needed for your health, then you make me get better, too. Take it easy and at your own speed. So, I decree: you did the right thing when you took care of your arm. I didn't do so badly myself today in bed,[1] from one o'clock on, because I got almost all the way through ten similes. I pick you as my sidekick and sergeant[2] on the ninth one, because it wasn't so successful at succumbing[3] to me. It's the one where "on the island of Aenaria there is a lake: in that lake there is another island, and it, too, is inhabited. *Allons, faisons-nous une comparaison comme ça.*"[4] Good-bye, my sweetest soul. My Lady says hello.

Notes

1. in bed: Marcus sometimes notes to Fronto that he is in bed when he writes; this is not a common practice among Roman letter writers (see also letters 7, 31, 38, and 39). He is writing at "the seventh hour," i.e., between 1:00 and 1:30 p.m. (depending on the time of year, which this letter doesn't specify).

2. sergeant: Lat. *optionem,* i.e., a junior officer chosen for some duty by a centurion or decurion.

3. successful at succumbing: Marcus puns on *secunda . . . persequor,* "favorable/following" and "follow, obey."

4. *Allons . . . comme ça:* Lit. "We make a simile out of this." These words are in Greek in the original.

Letter 5

MARCUS TO FRONTO, OCTOBER, ? 139-42 CE

Hi, my very best teacher,

I know that on each man's birthday his friends offer good wishes[1] for the man whose birthday it is; but because I love you next to my own self, I want to make a wish for myself on this day, your birthday. So all the gods who provide their present and ready strength for people anywhere in the world, who have the power to help us either by dreams or mysteries[2] or medicine or oracles in any way, each and every one of these gods I summon by my wishes, and I take my stand—depending on what kind of wish it is—in the place where the god in charge of each of them might hear me most easily.

And so before all I climb the citadel of Pergamum[3] and pray to Aesculapius[4] to steer the health of my teacher straight and watch over it awfully well. From here I go down to Athens, and on bended knee I beseech and beg Minerva that whatever I may ever learn about letters should above all journey from Fronto's mouth to my heart.[5] Now I return to Rome, and I call on the gods of roads and voyages with wishes that every trip I take may be with you beside me, and that I may not be worn out so frequently by such ferocious[6] longing. In the end I ask all the guardian gods of all the nations, and Jupiter himself, who thunders over the Capitol Hill,[7] to grant us that I should celebrate this day, on which you were born for me, along with you, and a happy, strong you.

Good-bye, my sweetest and dearest teacher. Please take care of your body so that when I come I'll see you. My Lady says hello.

Notes

1. good wishes: Marcus here is talking about a Roman custom of literally making a vow to a god on behalf of a friend; the closest Western equivalent now might be lighting a candle in church.

2. mysteries: Secret rituals, held to confer salvation on the participants.

3. Pergamum: Troy (in modern Turkey).

4. Aesculapius: The god of health.

5. to my heart: This is a poignant wish, given that, in the first book of his *Meditations,* written in his old age, Marcus lists Fronto indifferently and late among a crowd of other teachers and gives him no special intellectual credit.

6. so frequently by such ferocious: Lat. *tam saepe tam saevo.* Marcus is fond of jingles; cf. the words translated "steer the health of my teacher straight and watch over it awfully well" above. The Latin is *valetudinem magistri mei bene temperet vehementerque tueatur;* note the alliteration.

7. Jupiter himself: The text has *ipsum lucum,* "the grove itself"; *Iovem,* "Jupiter," is a conjecture. The Capitoline Hill in Rome was the site of the temple of Jupiter Best and Greatest.

Letter 6

FRONTO TO MARCUS, ? 139–42 CE

To my Lord,

Everything is fine with us when you are praying for us,[1] and of course no one is more worthy than you to get whatever he asks from the gods—unless that, when I pray for you, no one else is more worthy than you to have things gotten for him. Good-bye, my sweetest Lord. Say hello to your Lady.

Note

1. praying for us: This letter is taken to be the response to letter 5; if so, it is surprisingly reticent.

Letter 7

MARCUS TO FRONTO, ? 140–42 CE

Hi, my very best teacher,

How can I study when you're in pain, especially when you're in pain on account of me? Shouldn't I want to beat myself up and subject myself to all kinds of unpleasant experiences? God, I deserve it. After all, who else gave you that pain in your knee, which you write got worse last night, who else brought it on, if not Centumcellae,[1] if not me? So what am I supposed to do, when I don't see you and I'm tormented by such anguish? On top of this, even if I felt like studying, the court cases keep me from it, which, as people say who ought to know, eat up whole days. Still I've sent you today's slogan[2] and the day before yesterday's theme.[3] Yesterday we wore away the whole day on the road. Today it's hard to get anything done besides the evening slogan. You're saying, "Sleep'st thou so long a night?"[4] I certainly can sleep, because I'm a big sleeper; but it's so cold in my bedroom that I can hardly put my hands outside the covers. But in fact this is what's driven my mind most away from studying—that because I love letters too much I was a pain to you at the Port,[5] as this thing proves. So good riddance to all the Catos and Ciceros and Sallusts[6] just as long as *you're* good and I see you strong again, even without our books. Good-bye,[7] my number one delight, my sweetest teacher. My Lady says hello. Send me three slogans and some themes.

Notes

1. Centumcellae: The site of a villa in Etruria, on the coast northwest of Rome, owned by Antoninus Pius.

2. slogan: Gk. *gnomê* (= Lat. *sententia*), an epigrammatic turn of phrase, a neat way of putting an idea; one of the building blocks of declamation, hence something students had to make for exercise.

3. theme: Lat. *locus communis,* "commonplace," a topic that can be used in any speech: an expression of patriotism, a description of a storm or a quiet night, a vignette of the family hearthside or the happy farmer or the Golden Age (see, e.g., letter 11). Commonplaces were used as filler in speeches, but listeners gave points for an original take, so students had to practice them.

4. "Sleep'st thou so long a night?": Lat. *nocte . . . tam longa dormis.* This odd expression (= "Do you go to bed so early?") somewhat recalls Catullus 5.6, *nox est perpetua una dormienda,* "we must sleep one perpetual night"; hence here translated into poetic diction.

5. the Port: Centumcellae.

6. Catos and Ciceros and Sallusts: Cato = Marcus Porcius Cato (second century BCE), known as "the elder Cato," a Roman statesman and orator who rose to be censor, then the highest Roman office. He was noted for his stern, old-fashioned morality, professed hatred of all things Greek (despite an evident familiarity with the rules of rhetoric), and pithy prose style. His book *On Agriculture* is still extant (Marcus is reading it in letter 39); his speeches survive only in fragments. Cicero = Marcus Tullius Cicero (first century BCE), the greatest Roman orator, many of whose speeches, essays, and letters survive. Sallust = Gaius Sallustius Crispus (first century BCE), an unsuccessful politician and soldier who took to writing history, in an archaizing style that imitates Cato. Fronto loved the old-fashioned style for its clarity and rich vocabulary, and was trying to drum this taste into Marcus, with mixed success; thus Cato appears in letters 7, 11, 18, 23, 25, 27, 30, 33, 36, 38, and 39 (and see n. 3, letter 19), Sallust in letters 7 and 27.

7. good riddance . . . good . . . Good-bye: Marcus plays on *valere,* "good-bye/be off/be well."

Letter 8

Aurelius Caesar to his Fronto, hello,

I know you've often said to me that you want to know what you could do to please me most. The time is now here; now you can add to my love for you, if it can be added to. The trial[1] is coming up, and it seems that people are not going to be listening to your speech only with goodwill;[2] they'll be watching your display of indignation[3] with hostility. And I don't see anybody who would dare to warn you about this, because people who are less friendly to you actually like to see you acting more erratically; people who are more friendly are afraid they might seem to be better friends with your opponent if they distract you from your independent prosecution of him. And then if you've been mulling over some fancy turn of phrase for the case, they can't bear you to be deprived of your style through a deliberate silence. So, though you might think I have a lot of nerve to advise you or that I'm a brash little boy or too nice to your adversary, that won't make me drag my heels more in advising you to do what's right in my judgment. But why am I saying "advise"? I claim it from you and claim it earnestly and promise in return that, if I get what I ask for, I'll be obligated to you. But you'll say, "What? If I'm attacked, won't I pay him back in similar language?" But you'll gain more praise for yourself out of this if you don't make any response even if you are attacked. Of course if he does it first, people will be able to forgive you for responding however you want; but I've claimed it from him, too, not to start up, and I believe I've gotten what I ask. I really cherish both of you, each for his own merits, and I'm conscious that he was trained in the home of my grandfather Publius Calvisius,[4] but that I've been trained by you.[5] As a result I have the greatest concern in my heart that this extremely hateful business should be transacted in the most extremely honorable way it can be. I wish you'd approve of my strategy, for you'll be approving what I want. I've definitely chosen to not play it smart and write more, rather than be less of a friend and keep my mouth shut. Good-bye, my Fronto, dearest and most loving.[6]

Notes

1. The trial: This was probably the trial in which the Athenians brought claims against Tiberius Claudius Herodes Atticus for money owed them according to the terms of the will of Herodes' father. Herodes, an upper-class Greek who had been raised in Rome from the age of six, was a glamorous, wealthy philanthropist and noted sophist (a public speaker who also taught). His father was the first Greek to serve as consul in Rome, and Herodes himself was consul in 143 CE. He is a recurring figure in Philostratus's *Lives of the Sophists* (see esp. Wright 1952, 87–89, 119–25, 133–35, 139–83, 185). Letter 9 makes it clear how Fronto felt about Herodes; letters 8–10 provide a useful background for letter 34, written some years later to Herodes at Marcus's request. Note that Marcus never names Herodes here.

2. with goodwill: Lat. *benigne*. Marcus's wording leaves some ambiguity as to whether he is worried about the audience's attitude toward Fronto or its attitude toward Herodes—probably both.

3. display of indignation: This was a formal part of a speech. Marcus seems to be worried that Fronto will be too vehement because too sincere, and letter 9 shows that he is right to be worried.

4. Publius Calvisius: Marcus's maternal grandfather. Like other upper-class children from outside Rome, Herodes was brought by his father to a Roman aristocratic family and left there to be trained.

5. trained by you: This pretty conclusively anchors this letter in the period before Herodes became one of Marcus's teachers.

6. most loving: Lat. *amicissime*.

Letter 9

FRONTO TO MARCUS, 140–42 CE

Fronto to my Lord Caesar,

With good reason I've devoted myself to you, with good reason I've settled all my right to enjoy my life in you and your father.[1] What could be more like a friend, what more delightful, what more true?[2] Please, lose the "brash little boy" and "a lot of nerve."[3] As if there were any danger of you trying to talk me into something childishly or inadvisedly! Believe me if you want to—if not, I believe myself—the prudence of your elders is far outdone by you. I finally get it—when it comes to that business, your strategy is gray haired and weighty, while mine is really childish.[4] Of course, what need is there to put on a show for people, whether they're fair or unfair? If this Herodes person turns out to be a good and decent[5] man, it isn't telling the truth for a man like that to be bombarded with insults by me; if he is[6] worthless and indecent,[7] a contest between him and me isn't fair, and it can't lower his value. Of course every time you hug someone unclean you get dirty,[8] even if you come out on top. But the first point is truer, that a man you yourself judge worthy of your guardianship[9] is a decent man. If I had ever known about this, then may all the gods strike me dead if I would ever have dared to hurt any friend of yours with a word of mine.

Now, considering your love for me, which I feel so lucky to have,[10] I'd like you to help me with your strategy on this point as well. That I shouldn't say anything irrelevant to the case just to wound Herodes, I don't doubt. But some things in the case—and I have to say they're extremely heinous—how should I handle them? This is the thing I'm doubtful about, and I'm asking for a strategy. I have to talk about free persons cruelly beaten and stripped, one even killed, truly; I have to talk about a disloyal[11] son and one who forgot his own father's prayers; barbarity and greed must be exposed; a certain person[12] must be identified as an executioner.[13] But if with charges like these, which the case depends on, you think I ought to press my opponent and go after him with my best resources, please let me know what your strategy would be, best Lord, sweetest to me. If you truly think there should be some leniency even for things like this, whatever you recommend, that's what I'll think is best to do. You can rest assured, though, about one thing, as I've said—that I'll be saying nothing irrelevant to the case about his morals and the other areas of his life.[14] But if it does seem to you that I ought to serve my case, I'm warning you now that the use I'll be making of the occasion provided by this case couldn't even be called "unrestrained," for the charges are heinous and they have to be described in heinous terms. Those points I mentioned about persons wounded and stripped will come out of my mouth tasting of gall and bile; so if at some point I call him an "ignorant little Greek,"[15] it won't be cause for a fight to the death.

Good-bye, Caesar, and love me the most, as you do. I truly love to pieces every little letter of every word you write,[16] so I wish you would write me by your own hand whenever you write to me.[17]

Notes

1. and your father: Van den Hout (1999, 98) suggests that this indicates that Fronto sees Antoninus Pius behind Marcus's request.

2. more true: Lat. *verius.* This is probably a pun on Marcus's boyhood name, Marcus Annius Verus; Hadrian is said to have nicknamed him *Verissimus,* which means "very true" (*HA Life of Marcus* 1.10). Forms of *verus* pop up throughout the letter, often with some degree of sarcasm; cf. the repetition of Marcus's *consilium,* "plan," "strategy," from letter 8. Fronto seems to be gritting his teeth here, and the whole interchange in letters 8–10, as in letters 11–12, makes it clear who has the whip hand.

3. "brash little boy" . . . "a lot of nerve": Fronto is here responding to Marcus's words in letter 8.

4. I finally . . . childish: Another role reversal; cf. letter 3.

5. decent: Lat. *pudicus,* which has strong overtones of "sexually pure" (on norms for Roman male sexuality, see the volume introduction). Throughout the letter, Fronto uses sexually charged language in disparaging Herodes, a standard tactic in the rhetorical schools (see Richlin 1997).

6. is: There is a marked difference in the verb mood that Fronto chooses for the alternatives about Herodes' character: the good Herodes is in the subjunctive, the bad Herodes in the indicative.

7. indecent: Lat. *improbus,* a word with some sexual overtones.

8. every . . . dirty: Lit. "every embrace with someone ceremonially impure defiles you"; i.e., "lie down with dogs, get up with fleas"; or translate "if you have sex with someone diseased, you get infected"? The language that Fronto chooses to express this idea is highly charged: *complexus* really means "embrace" as in "putting your arms around" and can also mean "sexual intercourse"; *polluto,* here translated "unclean," has a range of meanings that includes "foul, infected, defiled with illicit sexual intercourse"; and *commaculat,* here "get dirty," has a range of meanings that includes "stain, contaminate, sully one's reputation." The image comes from Greek and Roman ideas about the necessity for abstinence from sex before performing religious rites; for the idea of contamination by contact, see, e.g., Plautus *Poenulus* 349–50. Juvenal's second satire, an attack on sex between adult males, uses the image of one diseased pig contaminating the rest of the herd (2.78–81).

9. guardianship: Another role reversal; fatherless boys up to the age of puberty had *tutores,* "guardians." Here Fronto depicts Marcus as Herodes' *tutor.*

10. which . . . have: This perhaps indicates Fronto's feeling that holding back on Herodes is a quid pro quo.

11. disloyal: Lat. *impio.* To a Roman, *pietas,* the loyalty and love owed between family members, is one of the highest virtues. The loyalty/love that a son owes his father is especially important; *filio impio* is tantamount to "wicked son."

12. a certain person: Obviously Herodes. Herodes' name does appear in the text after the word *quidam* (a certain [person]) but is probably a gloss (an ancient editor's note) that has crept into the text.

13. executioner: Lat. *carnufex.* This is an extremely insulting word; it literally means "flesh-maker" and is the title of a job that involved the torture and execution of slaves and the execution (by strangling) of the occasional citizen convicted of a capital crime. *Carnufex* connotes impurity (on defilement, see n. 8). This name-calling is somewhat ironic, since Fronto's first step on the career ladder was as *triumvir capitalis,* member of a board in charge of executions and prisons (Champlin 1980, 79). The charges listed so colorfully here by Fronto are par for the course in the Roman rhetorical schools, as in the *Controversiae* of the elder Seneca; the case at issue basically just dealt with money and the terms of a will.

14. I'll be . . . life: This promise did not limit Fronto much; Roman ideas of what was relevant to a case in terms of character assassination were highly elastic.

15. little Greek: Lat. *Graeculus.* This diminutive is an ethnic insult, used most famously by Juvenal (*Satires* 3.78), but also by Cicero. The tone is harsh, like that of *Spic* or *Hebe.* Elite Roman attitudes toward Greeks combined a mania for Greek culture with a contempt for Greek persons—ironic coming from Fronto (on Fronto writing as an African/outsider, see letter 21).

16. every . . . write: Lat. *etiam literulas tuas;* here clearly letters of the alphabet, not epistles.

17. so . . . whenever you write to me: Note the implication that Fronto has come to expect Marcus to write in his own hand (cf. letters 12, 18, 22, 32, 33, 40, and 41). Letter 8 does sound official—and carefully worded.

Letter 10

Hi my dearest Fronto,

So now here's to you, Fronto dearest—thanks, and I do feel grateful that you not only didn't reject my strategy but even okayed it.[1] But about those strategies you suggest in your extremely loving[2] letter, I think as follows. Everything that's relevant to the case you're in charge of obviously has to be brought out; what's relevant only to your own private feelings, even if they're justified and you've got provocation, still has to be kept quiet. And so you won't hurt your credibility in some dreary-midnight[3] business or damage your reputation for self-restraint . . . [illegible, about thirty-four characters] and let them say what <they like since> this one worry troubles me the most: I don't want you to say anything that might seem to be unworthy of your character, or irrelevant to the business, or blameworthy[4] to the bystanders. Good-bye, my Fronto, dearest and most delightful[5] to me.

Notes

1. okayed it: As if Fronto had a choice. This letter replies to letter 9.

2. extremely loving: Lat. *amicissime.*

3. dreary-midnight: Gk. *pannychio,* "all-night," written in the Roman alphabet. Van den Hout (1999, 105) translates as *totally gloomy, wretched.* But perhaps it truly just means "going on all night"? The term *pannychio* in Greek religion describes all-night rituals, and is not used elsewhere in Latin, although there is a character in Petronius's *Satyricon* called "Pannychis" (a seven-year-old girl whose defloration the protagonists watch, *Sat.* 25–26). The word also occurs in *Iliad* 2.24, "A counsel-bearing man should not sleep all night long," a line that is quoted by Marcus in a letter to Fronto in praise of not sleeping (*insomnia*) and against sleep (Haines 1.94–95 = *M. Caes.* 1.4 = van den Hout, p. 7, line 13), probably written in 143. Marcus there says jokingly that Fronto has done a rendition of this line, with others he quotes; letter 10, then, may also be teasing Fronto about this. Van den Hout (1999, 19) points out that *Iliad* 2.24 was much quoted by rhetoricians, but does not connect the letter against sleep with letter 10. The Poe-inspired translation here assumes Marcus feels the word as poetic and connects it

with night work; see n. 2, letter 1. But it is possible that this word is just a manuscript error or a misreading, hiding something that would make more sense.

4. blameworthy: Lat. *reprehensibile,* appearing here in Latin for the first time.

5. most delightful: A favorite term of Marcus's and a mark of his style. Compare Catullus 14.1–2: "If I didn't love you more than my eyes, / most delightful Calvus . . ."

Fronto to my Lord,

Since I know how worried you are . . . [two pages are missing]
<sheep> and doves followed him with wolves and eagles as he sang,
forgetful of traps and claws and teeth.[1] This story, to people who
read it rightly, certainly means this: there was a man of outstanding
intelligence and exceptional eloquence who bound many, many
people by their amazement at his virtues and fluency; he taught his
friends and followers in such a way that although they were immi-
grants of diverse races, with varying customs ingrained in them,
they still lived together in harmony and got used to each other and
flocked together, the gentle with the fierce, the calm with the violent, the restrained with the arrogant, the timid with the cruel; then
little by little they all stripped off their rooted vices, they followed
after virtue, they studied decency together, and exchanged shame-
lessness for a sense of shame, stubbornness for obedience, malice for
kindness. So if anybody ever had such strength of mind as to join[2]
his friends and followers among themselves in mutual love, you will
surely bring this about much more easily, since you were born with
all the virtues before you were taught them. After all, before you
were old enough to be taught, you were already mature, perfected
in all good qualities: before puberty a "good man," before you put
on a man's toga[3] "skilled in speaking."[4] Truly of all your virtues this
is perhaps the most amazing one, that you join all your friends in
harmony. Still I won't pretend that this isn't much more difficult
than taming wild beasts and lions with a lyre—and you'll more easily achieve it if you'll take care to utterly uproot and dig out this one
vice: don't let your friends be envious and either look spitefully at
each other or each think that your favor or kindness to another is a
loss and deprivation to himself. Spite is a destructive evil among human beings and the one that most often leads to a fight to the death,
equally harmful to itself and to others; but if you banish it far away

from your troops,[5] you'll have harmonious and kind friends, as you now do. But if it gets in somehow, it'll have to be extinguished with a lot of trouble and a lot of effort.

But please, let's chat about better things. I love Julianus[6]—actually this conversation has overflowed from the one I had with him; I love everyone who loves you dearly; I love the gods who watch over you; I love life because of you; I love letters[7] with you; <from> your <letters>[8] I engulf myself in your love.

Notes

1. <sheep> . . . teeth: The story of Orpheus, the great poet of Greek myth. Orpheus was famous for his ability to control the world through his words, for the loss of his wife Eurydice, and for rejecting all women in favor of boys after her death. Compare letter 21, in which it is himself to whom Fronto compares Orpheus. The wording of this letter puts a certain emphasis on Marcus as *vir*, "adult male," which he only barely was; this whole sequence of letters seems to be struggling with the question of relative power. It seems likely, therefore, that letter 11 is close in time to letter 10.

2. join: Lat. *copularet*, "link together"; repeated below.

3. before you put on a man's toga: It is tempting to translate this phrase as *before your bar mitzvah.* Roman boys, during the festival of the Liberalia (March 15) that came after they reached puberty, went through a ceremony in which they took off the boy's toga, the *toga praetexta,* and put on the man's toga, the *toga virilis,* for the first time; they were then escorted to the Forum by their fathers in a public display of their new status. Marcus took on the *toga virilis* "in his fifteenth year" (*HA Life of Marcus* 4.5), so probably in March 136 CE.

4. "good man" . . . "skilled in speaking": A famous quotation from the elder Cato, who defined the orator for his son Marcus as "a good man skilled in speaking." For Cato, see n. 6, letter 7.

5. troops: Lat. *cohorte,* i.e., a small group within the army or navy. The emperor's retinue of followers was so labeled by historians.

6. Julianus: There is no evidence as to which of a half dozen Julianuses this might be—possibly the eminent legal expert Publius Salvius Julianus. Whoever he is, he is clearly not a friend of Fronto's at this point.

7. I love letters: Lat. *litterae,* "letters" = (a) individual letters of the alphabet, (b) an epistle, or (c) literature. The English usage derives from this and well renders Fronto's indeterminate meaning here; cf. Marcus at the end of letter 7.

8. <from> your <letters>: Lat. <*ex epistulis*>, Haines's conjecture.

Letter 12

\<Hi my\> dearest \<teacher\>,

Although I'm coming to you tomorrow, still I can't bear to write nothing back, not even this tiny little bit, when your letters were so loving, so delightful, and so elegant, too, my own dearest Fronto. But what should I love first? What should I first say thank you for? Should I put it down first on my list, that while you were busy with so many projects at home and with so much public business, you still made the effort to go see my friend Julianus?[1]—and all for me—I'd be an ingrate if I didn't understand that. "But that's no big deal." Oh yes it is, if you throw in the rest—that you stuck around there for such a long time, that you had such a long chat, and a chat about me, or whatever would make him feel better; that you made a sick man more comfortable, and a friend more friendly to me; and on top of that you wrote me about every bit of this; and in that letter you gave me the news I wanted to hear about Julianus himself, the sweetest words, the healthiest advice. Why would I conceal from you what I can't conceal anyway? Even the very fact that you wrote me such a long letter, when I was going to be there tomorrow—that was really by far what I liked most of all: with this I personally thought I was the happiest person in the world, because with this you showed me so much and so sweetly how much you think of me and what trust you have in my friendship. What should I add, unless it's that I love you as you deserve? But what do I mean, "as you deserve"? I only wish I could love you as you deserve! And that's why I'm often angry with you when you're away, and I get so mad, because you won't let me love you as I want to, that is, you won't let my spirit follow the love of you up to its highest peak.

About Herodes,[2] go on with what you're saying, please; as our friend Quintus[3] says, "Once more unto the breach, dear friends." Not only does Herodes love you, but I'm working on this with you, and anybody who doesn't love you surely doesn't understand you in his mind or see you with his eyes; obviously I don't say a thing about ears, because everybody's ears slave under your whisper like prisoners of war.[4] To me this day seems longer than a day in spring and the night that's coming will seem wider than a winter night. For not only do I want more than anything to say hello to my Fronto, I especially want to put my arms around the writer of these last letters.

I wrote these lines to you on the run because Maecianus[5] was pushing me and your brother[6] needed to get back to you sooner rather than later—fair enough. So please, if a word here seems kind of ridiculous or an idea kind of half-baked or the writing kind of wobbly,[7] chalk it up to the lack of time. After all, though I love you so terribly much as my friend, I still ought to remember that as much love as I owe my friend, that's how much respect I should give my teacher. Good-bye, my Fronto, my dearest, and above all things the sweetest.

The *Sota-Guy* of Ennius[8] that you sent back to me seems to be on purer paper and a more charming book roll[9] and in gayer lettering than it was before. Gracchus[10] can wait with the barrel of new wine until we get there, and of course there's no fear that Gracchus will ferment along with the wine in the meantime. Good-bye, ever my sweetest soul.

Notes

1. Julianus: See letter 11.

2. Herodes: See letters 8–9. The first half of letter 11 must have discussed him, and from this letter it seems that Fronto had not yet come to think positively of him. This suggests a date for letter 12 after the trial of Herodes but before letters 32 and 34, not that letter 34 is all that positive.

3. Quintus: Probably Quintus Ennius. One of the early Roman writers (second century BCE) favored by Marcus and Fronto (see letters 22, 33, 44), he was known for his fondness for alliteration; the Latin quoted here is *pervince pertinaci pervicacia,* lit. "stand forth with stubborn steadfastness." He wrote epic poetry and drama as well as other forms of literature (see below in this letter). Marcus's reference here to "Quintus" is equivalent to a letter writer today referring to "our friend William" when discussing Shakespeare. To convey a similar tone, I have used a tag from Shakespeare (*Henry V* 3.1.1) in translating the quotation from Ennius that follows.

4. prisoners of war: Lit. "driven under the yoke," referring to a ceremony in which defeated soldiers were made to march under a wooden yoke.

5. Maecianus: The famous lawyer Lucius Volusius Maecianus, another of Marcus's teachers.

6. brother: Fronto's brother was named Quintus Cornelius Quadratus.

7. wobbly: Marcus draws attention to the fact that the letter is written by his own hand (cf. letters 9, 18, 22, 32, 33, 40, 41).

8. the *Sota-Guy* of Ennius: A reference to a lost work, known only in fragments (see Courtney 1993, 4–7). Sotades, a Greek, was the legendary originator of a type of verse named after him. This verse form is said to have had, not only a particular format, but also a particular content—the description of the goings-on of *cinaedi* (on whom see the volume introduction)—and, indeed, this is true of the fragments that we have from Ennius's *Sota*. The title *Sota* is a pet-name short form of the name Sotades, hence *Sota-Guy* here; an equivalent would give the tone better, e.g., *Bosie* or *Tru*. Other writers also cite it by this title—this isn't a joke of Marcus's.

9. book roll: The shape of Roman books—a cylinder with a boss at either end—occasionally inspired a joke in which the book is compared to a phallus (see Richlin 1992, 111; also Martial 11.6.14–16, a drunken offer of a book roll— "Catullus's Sparrow"—to a boy cupbearer in return for "Catullan kisses"). A similar joke seems present in the *Phaedrus,* where Socrates teases Phaedrus to tell him what he has in his left hand under his cloak (228d). For a remarkable example in the literary letters of the younger Seneca (an author disliked by Fronto but quoted by Marcus), see Habinek 1998, 145; Seneca makes the letter itself phallic. Letters could be cylindrical papyrus rolls as well as flat tablets (see the volume introduction).

10. Gracchus: Gaius Sempronius Gracchus (second century BCE), an early Roman orator and famous assassinated politician (see letter 13). He was known for his exciting style; maybe Marcus means he is fermented already. Cicero says of him that, in his speeches to the people (as opposed to speeches to the senate) he used a "much easier and freer level of speech" (*Brutus* 333). For Fronto's efforts to drum this idea into Marcus—from the letters, you wouldn't think he needed it, but evidently so—see letter 20. Gracchus appears in letters 12, 13, and 33.

Letter 13

MARCUS TO FRONTO, ? 142 OR EARLY 143 CE

His own Caesar to his teacher,

How much reading those speeches of Gracchus[1] helped me there's no need for me to say, since you would know best of all—you're the one who encouraged me to read them, with that so learned brain and that so kind nature of yours. But just so your book shouldn't come back to you all by itself with nobody to keep it company, I've sent this little nothing book[2] along with it. Be well, my sweetest teacher, most loving friend; I'm going to owe you whatever I'll ever know of letters.[3] I'm not such an ingrate that I don't understand what you've given me, when you've showed me your own notebooks[4] and when you don't stop leading me down the trail of truth every day and "opening my eyes," as people say. I love you as you deserve to be loved.

Notes

1. Gracchus: See n. 10, letter 12.

2. this little nothing book: Lat. *libellum istum*. Haines takes this to refer to the letter itself, but it might equally refer to a small book, as, e.g., at Catullus 1.1. Compare letter 38, where Marcus uses the word *libellos* of his own books.

3. whatever I'll ever know of letters: On Marcus's later change in attitude, see n. 5, letter 5.

4. notebooks: Fronto's *excerpta*—passages he has copied out of books for his own use (or has had copied for him), not an uncommon habit among Roman men of letters (cf. Marcus in letter 22).

Letter 14

Marcus Caesar to my teacher Fronto,

What can I possibly say about this rotten luck of mine, or how can I find words to blame these extremely hard circumstances that keep me tied up here with such an anxious heart, shackled by so much worry, and that don't let me run at once to my Fronto, to my most beautiful soul, especially in such an illness[1]—to come near, to hold his hands, and at least to give that foot a sensitive massage, as much as it can be done without hurting it, and to do some coddling in the bath, and to have him lean on my hand as he walks. And you call me your friend, when I don't drop everything and fly to you on the run? I'm the one who's truly lame, with this bashfulness of mine, no, my sluggishness. I should be—what should I say! I'm afraid to say something you may not want to hear, for you've certainly always worked in every way to keep me from worrying, with your jokes and your utterly charming words, and to show that you can endure all this and stay calm. But where my spirit may be, I don't know; except that I know this, that it's set out for that unknown place—to you.[2] Have pity, take care you get rid of this awful illness that you have to bear, because you're so brave, with all kinds of restraint and self-denial, while for me it's so truly harsh and utterly wicked.

Please write me right away all about what spa[3] you're setting off to and when, and how comfortably you're getting along now, and put my mind back in my body. Meanwhile I'll carry your letters around with me, even ones like these. Be well for me, my most delightful Fronto: though I ought to say it more organizedly—after all, you always <word missing> a lot: oh, all kind gods there are anywhere, I pray that my Fronto, most delightful and dearest to me, may get well: may he always be well with an unbroken, undiminished, uninjured body: may he be well and be able to be with me. Sweetest person, be well.

Notes

1. illness: Fronto, here and elsewhere, suffers from gout or arthritis. Note Marcus's use of foot imagery throughout.

2. that unknown place—to you: "O my America, my newfound land . . ." Commentators remark on the echo here of an early Latin pederastic epigram by Quintus Lutatius Catulus (consul 102 BCE), itself the subject of discussion by Aulus Gellius, Fronto's contemporary and acquaintance, who describes a dinner party at which one of the guests quotes it (Gellius 19.9, cf. 19.11.3; see Holford-Strevens 1988, 16–17; Richlin 1992, 39; Zetzel 2000; the Gellius stories make an extremely interesting context for this line, with their protagonists striving to prove the worth of erotic literature in Latin as opposed to Greek). Note that, in Catulus's epigram, the soul of the writer has flown out to his *erômenos*—Marcus, if he is alluding to this epigram, again here casts himself as *erastês*. On Fronto and pederastic epigram, see also n. 17, letter 44.

3. what spa: "waters," i.e., hot springs, mineral baths.

Letter 15

Fronto to his Caesar,

You, Caesar, love this Fronto of yours without limit, so that words scarcely suffice to you, such an eloquent person, to express your love and declare your kind feelings. What, I ask you, could be more fortunate, what could ever be luckier than me alone, to whom you send such burning letters? Why, you even say you want to run to me, to fly to me, as lovers do.

My Lady, your mother, often says as a joke that she's jealous of me because you hold me so dear. What if she were to read this letter of yours in which you even call on the gods and pray for my health? Oh lucky me, entrusted to the gods by your lips! Do you think that any pain would know how to penetrate my body or mind in the face of such joy? . . . [part of word missing] get better—wow! Now I feel no pain at all, I don't even feel ill: I'm strong, I'm healthy, I'm dancing; wherever you want me, I'll come; wherever you want me, I'll run. Believe me, I was suffused with such happiness that I couldn't write back to you at once; but I did send off the letters I'd already written in response to your earlier letter; I just held back the next courier, so I could come to my senses after this ecstasy.

And look, the night has gone by, and here it is, the next day, and indeed it's almost spent, and I still can't come up with what or how to respond to you. After all, what could I put down that would be more delightful, more alluring, more loving, than what you wrote to me? And so I'm glad that you've made me an ingrate, unequal to the task of repaying your favor, since, as things are, you love me so that I could hardly love you more.

So let me assign a topic for a longer letter: please tell me—what have I done to make you love me so? What has this Fronto person of yours done that's so good that you should hold him so dear? Did he ever risk his life for you or your parents? Did he throw himself in front of you all to save you from danger?[1] Did he faithfully administer some province? Did he lead an army? None of the above.

He doesn't even perform little daily services around you more than others do; really he has, if you want to know the truth, a pretty bad attendance record. After all, he doesn't come to your house every morning at daybreak, or make his formal greeting to you every day, or go with you everywhere, or always watch you.[2] So you see to it that, if anyone asks you why you love Fronto, you have something ready to give as a response.

But indeed I want nothing better than for there to be no reasoning behind your love of me.[3] Love doesn't seem to me to be love at all when it rises out of reasoning and is joined together[4] for justifiable and specific causes; I think of love as chancy and free and a slave to no causes, conceived by a violent impulse rather than by reasoning; it gets hot not from services rendered[5]—like a pile of firewood—but from steam that rises spontaneously. I like the hot grottoes of Baiae[6] better than any old bathhouse furnace,[7] where a fire is lit with expense and smoke and shortly goes out. But this purebred[8] steam is clean and constant, and charming and free of charge as well. By the very same token, those so-called friendships that heat up based on services rendered present their occasional smoke and tears, and the minute you stop, the fire is out; but chance love is both undiluted and delightful.[9]

And how about the fact that friendship born out of deserving deeds doesn't grow up or reach its full strength in the same way as that sudden and unplanned love does? Young trees cultivated and watered by hand in orchards and garden patches don't grow up as well as the oak and fir, the alder and cedar and spruce there on the mountains, which are born spontaneously, set out without reasoning and without order, and brought up by no labors or services of the cultivators but by the wind and rain.[10]

So that love of yours, sprung up without cultivation and without reasoning, will grow on up, I hope, with the cedars and oak trees: if it were cultivated for reasons depending on services rendered, it wouldn't grow higher than myrtle or laurel, which have plenty of scent but not much strength.[11] All in all, as much as chance prevails over reasoning, so chance love prevails over love based on services.

Come on—who doesn't know that "reason" is a word for human

planning, while Chance[12] is a goddess, and chief of the goddesses? Who doesn't know that temples, shrines, sanctuaries everywhere are dedicated to Chance, while to Reason not a statue or an altar is consecrated anywhere? So I'm not wrong to want your love for me to be born of chance and not reason.

Nor is reasoning ever truly the equal of chance, either in greatness or usefulness or importance. Clearly you wouldn't compare ramparts, built by human hand and reason, with mountains, or aqueducts with rivers, or reservoirs with springs. Then the "reason" behind our planning is called "prudence," while the impulses of prophets are known as "divination." But nobody would put more faith in the plans of the most prudent woman than in the prophetic chants of the Sibyl. To what end is all this leading? To say that I rightly prefer to be held dear because of impulse and chance than because of reason and my deserving deeds.

So if there is any justifiable reason for your love of me, Caesar, please let's take good care that it should be unknown and lie hidden. Let people doubt, talk, argue, guess, quest after the origin of our love, just like the sources of the Nile.[13]

But now the hour is touching four, and your courier is muttering. So let there be a limit to my letter. I'm actually feeling much more comfortable than I expected. I'm not thinking about the spa[14] at all any more. You, my Lord, jewel of the Roman way,[15] my consolation for bad times—how much do I love you? You'll say, "Not more than I love you?" I'm not such an ingrate that I'd dare to say so. Be well, Caesar, and your parents too, and cultivate that mind of yours.

Notes

1. throw . . . danger: Lit. "did he give himself as a *succidaneus* for your dangers?" A *succidaneus* was a substitute sacrificial victim. In the previous sentence, Fronto has asked whether he *caput . . . devovit*, lit. "pledged his head to death," referring to a type of ritual sacrifice (*devotio*) famous in Roman history, in which a soldier pledged his life to the gods of the dead in return for victory; stories told of how Decius Mus, for example, in order to win a key battle for Rome, plunged his horse into an abyss that opened up in the earth. For the second-century interest in quaint ritual practices, see Zetzel 2000.

2. he doesn't come . . . watch you: The duties in this sentence are those of a *cliens* (dependent person, client) to a *patronus* (patron); the relation between *patronus* and *cliens* was one of the foundations of Roman culture and went all the way up the social ladder from ex-slaves to kings. This is a conventional list (see Juvenal *Satires* 1.127–46, 3.119–89, 5.12–23, 6.312–13), with the exception of the last item, with its suggestion of the *patronus* as spectacle for the *cliens*. The list then also resembles the to-do list of an elegiac lover (as in the love elegies of Propertius, Ovid, et al.), who waits on and gazes at his beloved. Fronto's philosophy of love, then, marks him as romantic, if stiff, at times lawyerly, and careful to write in code.

3. But . . . me: This idea forms the basis of the rest of the letter. It looks back to the *erôtikos logos* of letter 2 and the idea of the superiority of the nonlover, but mostly it engages with Stoic ideas on love and friendship, which upheld reason over passion (see Gaca 2003, 60, and the volume introduction). The word translated here as "reason(ing)" is *ratio,* which also means "plan(ning)," "program," "theory."

4. is joined together: Lat. *copulatur.* The word usually refers to a physical join.

5. services rendered: This refers back to the performance of daily attendance above, here compared with sticks of kindling.

6. Baiae: A Roman resort on the Bay of Naples, famous for its hot springs and as a playground for the rich and famous.

7. bathhouse furnace: Public baths were a major feature of Roman culture and have left plentiful physical remains. They were part of daily life for everyone, although wealthy people sometimes had a bathhouse of their own attached to a country villa (see letters 35, 39). But bathhouses were also the site of some scenes of cruising in literature (see the sources listed in Richlin 1992, 276), and love is sometimes compared to a bathhouse attendant stoking the fires (see the love charm from Roman Egypt in Brooten 1996, 81–90). Moreover, the public baths charged admission, suggesting another subtext here: the stock comparison between sex with slave prostitutes and sex with free citizens (cf. "expense" here with "purebred" and "free of charge" in the next sentence). Indeed, "Baiae" suggests upper-class citizens in general—and in particular Marcus, who dates his essay against sleep from Baiae, possibly around this time. So, at one level, this simile means "I like Marcus better than any bathhouse slut." On the visual imagery of bathhouses and the African male as bathhouse attendant, see Clarke 1998, 119–42.

8. purebred: Lat. *ingenui,* used of natural features to mean "indigenous," but most commonly applied to people to mean "freeborn." Being born free is treated in Latin texts as something creditable.

9. undiluted and delightful: Fronto here and elsewhere in the letter uses a jingle: here *iugis et iucundus* (continuous/ever-flowing and delightful); cf. *puri*

perpetuique (clean and constant) and *grati . . . et gratuiti* (charming and free of charge) above and *satis odoris, parum roboris* (plenty of scent but not much strength) below. This is a feature of the so-called African style, common to Fronto and other Roman writers from Africa, most famously Apuleius.

10. Young trees . . . wind and rain: Like that of the bathhouse furnace (see n. 7 above), this simile seems to have two layers, at one level comparing love and friendship to trees and saplings, at another comparing Marcus to a young tree surrounded by "cultivators" and Fronto to the wild rain on the mountains. A repeated theme for Fronto, and the only one at all recalled by Marcus in the *Meditations* of his old age, was to warn Marcus of the insincerity and flattery of the courtiers around him, from whom Fronto wants to differentiate himself. The word *educantur*—here translated *brought up*—is used of children as well as of plants and animals. For a phallic "young tree in the hills," see Horace *Epodes* 12.20.

11. myrtle . . . strength: Myrtle and laurel are low-growing bushes. Both have associations with gods (Aphrodite and Apollo, respectively), and their branches were used to make wreaths for prizes in contests dedicated to those gods. The laurel in particular not only stands for literary inspiration but, because it features in the tale of Apollo and Daphne, recalls the story of a beauty pursued by a god who has rape in mind. *Daphne* in Greek means *laurel,* and the nymph Daphne turns into a laurel tree to escape Apollo. The trees of the mountain, on the other hand, have an association with the tree that grew on Mt. Pelion and was cut to make the keel of the *Argo* (the ship commanded by Jason in his quest for the golden fleece)—an event often cited in literature as (a) the beginning of a lot of trouble and (b) the first step in the doomed love story of Jason and Medea (or of several doomed love stories, see Catullus 64.1). On the use of a jingle here, see n. 9 above.

12. Chance: Fortuna.

13. Let . . . Nile: This sentence strongly recalls Catullus 7, in which the poet says that he and his mistress should put off the curious and ill-wishers by making their kisses as innumerable as the sands of the Libyan desert.

14. spa: Lit. "waters." Cf. letter 14, where Marcus asks Fronto what spa he plans to visit.

15. jewel of the Roman way: Lat. *decus morum,* lit. "ornament of/source of pride to the traditions/customs/virtues." *Mos* is used here in a peculiarly Roman sense: "what we do," "the right way to do things."

Letter 16

Hi my Fronto, deservedly dearest,

I understand that oh so clever pirouette[1] of yours, which you so very kindly came up with—that, since you didn't have credibility in praising me because of your outstanding love for me,[2] you were looking for credibility for your praise by berating me. But oh lucky me, to seem worthy both to be praised and to be chastised by my Marcus Cornelius, greatest of orators, best of men! What should I say about your kindest, truest, lovingest letter?[3] Well, "truest" up to the first part of your letter; for the rest, where you bestow your approval on me—as some Greek says, I think Thucydides,[4] "Love is blind, and lovers cannot see,"[5] and so you interpreted part of my stuff with almost a blind love. But—this is how much it means to me that I don't write correctly and that you praise me out of no merits of my own but only out of your love for me, which you just wrote so much to me about,[6] and so elegantly—I, if you want me to, will be something. Also your letter made sure that I now realize how terribly much you love me. But as for my lack of *esprit,*[7] my spirit is still just as shaky and a tiny bit sad in case I said anything today in the senate on account of which I might not deserve to have you as my teacher. Good-bye, my Fronto, my—what should I say but—very best friend.

Notes

1. pirouette: Marcus wrote *strofa,* evidently the Greek *strophê,* "turn," the technical term for a stanza of poetry, deriving from the "turn" taken by the chorus in a Greek play. It can just mean "twist."

2. since . . . me: This seems still to refer back to the *erôtikos logos*—specifically, to the section on lovers' credibility in praise of their beloveds (see letter 2).

3. your . . . letter: This may be referring to a letter (Haines 1.104–7 = *M. Caes.* 3.16 = van den Hout, pp. 49–50) in which Fronto says he could not sleep for wondering whether he has previously held off from critiquing Marcus's style out of *nimio amore,* "too much love," and goes on to give a critique. But letter 16 may be responding to a letter or letters of Fronto's not in the extant collection.

4. Thucydides: That's what the codex says. Haines substitutes Theophrastus because St. Jerome attributes this line to him; almost the same words occur at Plato *Laws* 731e. Marcus elsewhere seems to garble quotations, however, and it's very like him to attribute these words to the austere historian Thucydides (fifth century BCE), who never talks about love.

5. "Love . . . see": Lit. "Loving is blind about the thing loved." The words are in Greek in the original.

6. which . . . about: This may refer to letter 15.

7. lack of *esprit:* Gk. *athumia,* "lack of spirits."

Letter 17

My Fronto, the most magnificent consul,[1]

I give up, you win: you've clearly surpassed in loving all the lovers who have ever existed. Take your victory garland and let the herald announce publicly in front of your tribunal this big victory of yours: "The consul Marcus Cornelius Fronto is the winner and is crowned champion in the competition at the Olympics of *Amitié*."[2] But I—even though I'm defeated, I still won't give in or give up a bit of my *folie* for you.[3] Oh sure, teacher, so you'll love me more than any person ever loved another person; well, I, though I have less strength in loving, will truly love you more than any person loves you, more even than you love your very own self. Now the competition for me will be against Cratia,[4] though I'm afraid I can't beat her. After all, in her case, really, as Plautus says, "The storm of love hasn't just soaked her dress with its big raindrops but rained straight into the marrow of her bones."[5]

What kind of letter do you think you wrote me! I'd venture to say the woman who bore me and brought me up never wrote me anything so delightful, so honey-sweet.[6] And this wasn't the result of your gift with words or your eloquence; in that case not only my mother but everyone breathing would immediately yield to you— as they do. But that letter of yours that you wrote me wasn't just lucid and learned but bubbling with such kindness, overflowing with such feeling, shining with such love, I can't fully express how it raised up my soul on high with joy, how it spurred me on with the most burning desire, and finally, as Naevius says, filled my soul with "death-penalty love."[7]

That other message of yours, in which you were explaining why you were going to be a little late in making the senate speech in which you'll be praising my Lord,[8] filled me with such pleasure that I couldn't control myself—and you'll see if I did something that took nerve—I had to declaim it to my father[9] in person. And I don't have to spell out how much it pleased him, since you're well aware of his extreme kindness—also of the outstanding elegance of your letter. But out of this thing grew a long conversation between us about you, much, much longer than the one you and your quaestor[10] had about me. And so I don't doubt that your ears were burning right there in the forum for quite a while. So my Lord bestows his approval on you and loves the reasons why you've postponed your speech to a later day . . . . [manuscript breaks off]

Notes

1. consul: This term of address dates the letter securely to Fronto's two-month suffect consulship, July–August 143 CE, and the letter must have been written well before August 13 (see n. 8 below). On the suffect consulship, see n. 6, letter 26.

2. "The consul . . . *Amitié*": These words appear in Greek in the original. The name of the contest is given as "the Great Philotesia," a joking formation based on the names of religious festivals (Megalesia, Dionysia) that featured athletic and literary contests. *Philotês*, here translated "*Amitié*," is a term for *friendship*, but, like *amicitia*, it shares its root with a word for love (*philia*)—although this is not erotic love (see Konstan 1997).

3. my *folie* for you: Mixed Lat./Gk. *mea prothymia*. The Greek *prothymia* (transcribed in the manuscript into the Roman alphabet) is "eagerness/desire/enthusiasm" and in the context suggests a combination of sports fan–ship and having a crush.

4. Cratia: Fronto's wife.

5. Plautus . . . "the storm . . . bones": Plautus was an early Roman comic playwright (ca. 200 BCE). Twenty of his musicals are extant, but these exact words appear nowhere in them. In his *Mostellaria* (*Monster Time*), however, these words appear: "Love came right down . . . like a storm. / It has soaked right into my chest, it has got my heart all wet" (142–43). This is part of a memorable and catchy song in which a young man compares human beings to houses and himself in particular to a house where the owner has let the roof go. Scholars think that Marcus is either misquoting (maybe deliberately) but including part of the song that is lost, or just misquoting, or quoting another song from Plautus altogether, one now lost. If Marcus is misquoting from *Mostellaria*, it's a transgender misquotation along the lines of "She's singin' in the rain."

6. honey-sweet: Lat. *mellitum*, a word favored by Catullus, who uses it to describe his mistress's sparrow (3.6) and his beloved boy (48.1, 99.1).

7. Naevius . . . "death-penalty love": Naevius was another early Roman writer (second century BCE), a dramatist. The striking phrase *amore capitali*, "death-

penalty love," is not otherwise attested; the image seems to come directly from legal language.

8. my Lord: The emperor, Antoninus Pius, Marcus's adoptive father. The reference here is to Haines 1.108–13 = *M. Caes.* 2.1 = van den Hout, pp. 24–25, where Fronto promises the speech will be given on August 13.

9. my father: Antoninus Pius.

10. quaestor: Each consul had a junior magistrate called a *quaestor* assigned to him; quaestors were young men, so this was something of a mentor/protégé relationship.

Letter 18

To my teacher,

I've been writing from 10:30 to this hour and I've read a lot of Cato[1] and I'm writing this to you with the same pen[2] and I'm saying hello and I want to know how you're getting on. Oh how long it is that I haven't seen you . . . . [manuscript breaks off here]

Notes

1. Cato: Early Roman orator and statesman of the second century BCE (see n. 6, letter 7, and n. 3, letter 19). Marcus has written this letter in the paratactic style for which Cato was famous (on the paratactic style, see n. 6, letter 27).

2. pen: Lat. *calamo,* lit. "reed"; this indicates that Marcus was writing on papyrus. Note that this letter announces itself as autograph. On the mechanics of Roman letter writing, see the volume introduction, and cf. letters 9, 12, 22, 32, 33, 40, and 41.

Letter 19

MARCUS TO FRONTO, JULY–EARLY AUGUST, 143 CE

<Marcus Caesar to his teacher, consul most magnificent>,

. . . [letter begins from a break in the manuscript] it might seem.
We heard Polemo[1] declaiming three days ago, to have a *soupçon* of
chitchat about human beings as well.[2] If you want to know how
he seemed to me, just listen. Seems to me he's like a hardworking
farmer,[3] gifted with supreme shrewdness, who's covered a big farm
with a crop of only wheat and grapevines, where, sure, the harvest
is most flawless and the yield is most fruitful. And yet nowhere in
that country place is there a Pompey fig or Arician greens or a Tar-
entine rose[4] or a pleasant grove of trees or thick woods or a shady
plane tree;[5] everything is more for use than pleasure, and more what
has to be praised but you don't want to love.

OK, would I seem to have a fresh enough attitude and a lot of
nerve, when I'm critiquing a man with such a high reputation? But
when I remember I'm writing to you, I think I'm less daring than
you'd wish. We're getting ourselves awfully hot about this—hey,
that was a purebred hendecasyllable.[6] So before I start poetizing,[7]
I'm taking a break with you. <Good-bye>, most-longed-for person
and dearest to your True,[8] consul most magnificent, sweetest teacher.
Good-bye, always my sweetest soul.

Notes

1. Polemo: One of the greatest rhetoricians of the second century CE (see Gleason 1995). He comes up again in letter 20. For an ancient biography of Polemo including a story about Marcus's higher opinion of him at a later date, see Philostratus *Lives of the Sophists* 25 (trans. in Wright 1952, 107–37). Philostratus's account
makes it clear that Herodes Atticus studied with Polemo and was his enthusias-
tic supporter (see Wright 1952, 119–25); in that case, Fronto would have disliked
him (see letters 9 and 34), as perhaps tactfully anticipated by Marcus here.

2. to have . . . as well: These words are in Greek in the original.

3. like a hardworking farmer: The adjective *strenuus* strongly suggests that
Marcus is thinking here of the ideal farmer of Cato's *On Agriculture,* who is associated in that work's preface with being *strenuus,* and the whole metaphor re-

calls Cato's book—which we gather was at this point, along with Polemo, not much to Marcus's taste. Fronto has been trying to get Marcus to write in plain style (Haines 1.104–7 = *M. Caes.* 3.16 = van den Hout, pp. 49–50); for what Marcus does with such advice, see letter 18. Fronto picks up on *strenuus,* somewhat awkwardly, in letter 20.

4. Pompey . . . rose: All these are, evidently, instances of crops that give pleasure; the place-names are in Italy. The fig is called *Pompeianus* not because it came from the town of Pompeii but because it was actually named after Pompey, the Roman general (Pliny *Natural History* 15.70). It might be better to translate with equivalents: "A Macintosh apple or a California avocado or a Texas rose."

5. shady plane tree: See n. 5, letter 3. This phrase has a slight echo of Plato, Polemo's stylistic opposite; indeed, the critique of Polemo takes us back to the *Phaedrus* as well as to Cato (n. 3 above).

6. hendecasyllable: In the Latin, the previous clause follows the metrical pattern called a *hendecasyllable* (eleven-syllable), a favorite of Catullus and Martial. Marcus calls it *ingenuum,* which means "indigenous" when used of natural features and "freeborn," i.e., "nonslave, classy," when used of people (see n. 8, letter 15).

7. poetizing: Lat. *poetari,* a made-up word that Marcus borrows from Ennius's satires.

8. True: Marcus's boyhood name was Marcus Annius Verus; *verus* means "true" (see n. 2, letter 9).

Letter 20

To Caesar Aurelius my Lord, from your consul Fronto,

What an ear people have these days! What good taste they show as spectators of speeches! You'll be able to find out from our friend Aufidius[1] how many bravos it aroused during my speech,[2] and with what unanimous cries of approval they received my line "Then every family portrait[3] was painted with patrician emblems." But when I put together the noble class with the ignoble class and said, "As if a man were to think that fires lit from the funeral pyre and the altar were alike because they equally gave light," at this a couple of people started muttering.[4]

To what end have I told you about this? So that you might get yourself together,[5] Lord, when you come to make a speech to a group of folks, to be conscious that you have to be a slave to their ears—of course not everywhere and in every way, but at least sometimes and to some degree. When you do this, consider that you're doing something similar to what you both[6] do when you give out honors or their freedom to men who have worked hard[7] in killing beasts, when the people clamor for it.[8] They may even be wrongdoers or condemned for some crime, but when the people clamor for it, you give them what they want. And so the people everywhere lord it over us and hold the upper hand. And so—as it will please the people, so you will act and so you will speak.

Here it is, that greatest and most difficult virtue of an orator: to delight his listeners without much harm done to honest rhetoric. And this baby talk[9] he gets together to caress the ears of the crowd with should not be smeared on[10] any too indecently: better he should sin in the softness[11] of the composition and structure than in a shameless slogan.[12] I'd rather have clothing, too, be dainty in the softness of the wool than in its womanish color—in a thin or silken[13] fiber, but purple itself, not flame yellow or saffron.[14] Especially for the both of you, who are required to wear purple and scarlet,[15] your speeches, too, sometimes have to be dressed in the same style. You will do this thing, and you will balance and modify it in the best way and with the best kind of balance. And that's what I predict: whatever has ever been done in the field of rhetoric, you will bring it to perfection, you are gifted with such talent and you train yourself with such dedication and work—especially considering the other people who've gained an outstanding reputation either through dedication without talent or talent alone without dedication.

I'm sure, Lord, that you're also spending quite a bit of time on writing prose. After all, though the speed of horses is trained just as well if they run in their training at a gallop or a trot, still those things that are required more often must be practiced more frequently.

I'm obviously not dealing with you now as if I thought you were twenty-two years old. At an age when I had hardly laid a finger on any of the classical[16] texts, you have achieved, thanks to the gods and yourself, the kind of advanced ability in rhetoric that would be enough to make the reputation of senior men—and, what's the most difficult thing to do, in every level of discourse. After all, your letters, which you've written so regularly, show me well enough what you can also do in that more relaxed and Tullian[17] sort of thing.

Instead of the rhetorician Polemo,[18] whom you presented to me in your latest letter as Tullian, I, in the speech that I gave in the senate, portrayed the philosopher Polemo[19]—who, unless I'm deceived in my opinion, is quite an Attic one.[20] Well, what do you think, Marcus—how does the story of Polemo as set down by me seem to you? Obviously Horatius Flaccus[21] supplied me with a lot of witty things about this—a poet worth remembering and, because of Maecenas and my gardens (once owned by Maecenas), not unrelated to me.[22] Well, this Horace in the second book of his satires put in that story about Polemo, if I remember rightly, in these verses:[23]

Like Polemo transformed, would you take off your sickness's emblem—
the tight jeans, the ascot, the shades—as it is said of him:
that he was drunk, and sneakily picked the garlands off his neck,
when he was caught up by the learned man who hadn't had breakfast yet.

The verses you sent me I've sent back to you by way of our friend Victorinus,[24] and this is how I sent them back: I carefully sewed up the page with thread,[25] and I set my seal across the thread in such a way that that little mouse couldn't get into any cracks or crevices[26] anyhow. After all, he never shared anything from your hexameters[27] with me himself, he's so bad and wicked. But he says that you purposely declaim your hexameters at a fast and furious pace, and so he can't have them by heart. So now I've paid him back in kind, even-steven, so he won't hear any verse of yours from here. Also I remember that you've often warned me not to show your verses to anyone.

What's up, Lord? Surely you're happy, surely you're very well, above all surely you're in good shape. If only you don't ever shake us up the same way you shook us up on your birthday,[28] I won't get worked up about the rest. If you have a problem, *honi soit qui mal y pense!*[29] Good-bye my delight, in you I trust,[30] good-bye my happiness, my pride and joy. Good-bye and love me, please, in every style, joking or serious.

I've written a letter to your mother, and I'm so shameless,[31] I've written it in Greek, and I've folded it in with the letter addressed to you. You read it first, and, if there's any barbarism[32] in it, you who are fresher from Greek literature should correct it, and then give it to your mother. After all, I don't want your mother to look down on me as a hillbilly.[33] Good-bye, Lord, and give your mother a big kiss[34] when you give her the letter, so she'll read it more eagerly.

Notes

1. Aufidius: Gaius Aufidius Victorinus, a younger friend of Marcus's who would grow up to marry Fronto's daughter Cratia. He shows up again later in the letter and seems to be carrying letters back and forth between Marcus and Fronto.

2. my speech: Van den Hout (1999, 44–46) argues that this was not Fronto's big speech of thanks to the emperor in the senate (see n. 8, letter 17), but one given to the general public in June, before Fronto entered into his consulship. This would date the letter in early July, and would also make the beginning of the letter a natural introduction to the doomed argument that Fronto goes on to make to Marcus about the necessity for playing to the crowd (see further below).

3. family portrait: Lat. *imago.* Male Roman aristocrats had the right to have

life masks made of themselves. Families kept their masks in a special cupboard in the front hall of their mansions; generations' worth of such *imagines* were taken out on the occasion of a family funeral and worn as masks in the funeral procession (see Flower 2000).

4. started muttering: From Fronto's other remarks in the letter, it seems that what his audience liked and disliked depended on issues of style; the first line is terse and includes an alliteration, the second uses a simile and a faint jingle. Roman crowds were also said to be sensitive to the rhythm of oratorical prose. But the content of each line may also be at issue: each deals with Roman ideas about nobility, and possibly the second might have given offense as arrogant, especially if the speech was given to the general public (see n. 2 above). Fronto himself probably came from a wealthy but not a noble family.

5. get yourself together: Fronto makes a slight play on *comparans,* "comparing, putting together" (par. 1), and *compares,* "you might prepare," picked up by *comparat* in par. 3.

6. you both: Marcus and his father, the emperor Antoninus Pius.

7. worked hard: Lat. *strenue.* The adjective *strenuum* features in the preface of Cato's *On Agriculture* and, to readers of Cato like Marcus and Fronto, would connote old-fashioned rigor (but see n. 3, letter 19).

8. clamor for it: The situation envisioned is a scene at the wild-beast fights in the arena, when the emperor and prince would be exhorted by the cries of the crowd to reward one of the hunters, who were usually slaves or condemned criminals. This was an unfortunate analogy for Fronto to pick; a later historian records that Marcus particularly disapproved of bloody spectacles and refused to free the trainer of a man-eating lion (Dio 72.29.4). Moreover, the whole argument—that it is the job of the orator to pander to his audience, rather than to stick to the unvarnished truth—directly opposes the principles upheld by Plato, runs into the problem that Fronto set up for himself by starting with the *Phaedrus,* and paradoxically produces an error that illustrates its own point: Marcus's nickname, after all, was "Very True" (see n. 2, letter 9; letter 19 at n. 8).

9. baby talk: Lat. *delenimenta,* "sweet talk." This word shows up in a quotation from Laberius in letter 33; see nn. 11–12, letter 33.

10. smeared on: Lat. *fucata,* "dyed/stained/slathered with makeup"; the image is often used by writers on rhetoric. This whole section participates in an old argument wherein rhetoric is treated as gendered and the theorist decries wording and even syntax that are perceived as effeminate; the elements of effeminacy (*mollitia*) include wearing makeup, wispy clothing, and certain colors (see Richlin 1996, 1997).

11. softness: Lat. *mollitia* (see n. 10 above). In what follows, Fronto actually manages to advocate *mollitia* within limits, as part of the goal of seducing the

populace. Compare Lucian's satire *Rhêtorôn didaskalos* (*Teacher of Rhetoricians*), where this argument is made as a joke.

12. shameless slogan: Lat. *impudens,* "shameless," a word with sexual overtones associated with effeminacy in men or sluttishness. It is hard for us to understand how a *sententia* (a turn of phrase or an epigram, here translated as *slogan*) could be shameless (see letter 7), but consider how serious writers today talk about advertising or how the "legitimate stage" is contrasted with television. Fronto may have in mind the Roman equivalent of "It's morning in America" or "Mission accomplished." Fronto playfully refers to his own *impudentia* at the end of the letter.

13. silken: Cf. Juvenal *Satires* 2.65–78, where the satirist mocks an effeminate lawyer for wearing a see-through toga.

14. flame yellow or saffron: These colors were considered feminine because of their use in Roman bridal veils.

15. purple and scarlet: Emperors wore these high-prestige colors, as Roman citizen boys and senators traditionally wore them in the border of their togas. The dye was extremely expensive and hard to make.

16. classical: Lat. *veterum,* lit. "old" or "old-time." To a Roman—and especially to Marcus and Fronto, who loved early Latin style—old was always good (cf. letters 23, 33).

17. Tullian: Fronto here refers to Marcus Tullius Cicero as the model for all later letter writers. The style of letters was informal by comparison with the style of speeches.

18. the rhetorician Polemo: See letter 19. Marcus hardly makes Polemo sound "Tullian" in that letter. Van den Hout thinks this is sarcasm (1999, 52), but maybe there is something wrong with the text here; it should say "Catonian"—Cato-like. Or maybe letter 20 is not a response to letter 19.

19. the philosopher Polemo: The head of the Academy (Athens, late fourth century BCE) and the teacher of Zeno, the founder of Stoicism. He is said to have barged in on a meeting of the Academy while returning home one morning from a drunken all-night party, and to have been turned to a sober life of philosophy then and there by the words of Xenocrates (the "learned man" in the verses Fronto goes on to quote).

20. an Attic one: The original could also have read *an ancient one,* but a comment on things Attic would have more force between Marcus and Fronto than one on dates. See letter 3, and Marcus's comment on the rhetorician Polemo having no plane trees in letter 19.

21. Horatius Flaccus: One of the most famous Roman poets (first century BCE), he wrote lyric poetry, satire, and poetic epistles under the first emperor, Augustus. The way Fronto patronizes him here (Horace claimed to be the son of a freed slave)

is not unique; Fronto's older coeval the younger Pliny, who was a member of the upper class, does much the same with a whole list of poets (Richlin 1992, 7).

22. my gardens . . . unrelated to me: Maecenas was Horace's first patron, proverbial for his wealth (and effeminate literary style). Fronto's real estate purchase bespeaks his own great wealth and here enables him in effect to own both Horace and Maecenas.

23. in these verses: Horace *Satires* 2.3.254–57. At this point in Horace's satire, the narrator is being harangued by a Stoic convert about a lecture he has heard on the paradox "All men but the philosopher are mad," and, the harangue having moved to the subject of sexual madness, Polemo is given as an example of a person suddenly converted (ostensibly from dissipation to philosophy rather than from sexual madness to sobriety, although the distinction is blurry). Note that the symptomatic accessories (lit. "garters, elbow-cushions, and throat-warmers") are sported by the addressee and are thus those of a would-be sexy dude; these accessories in Latin have overtones both of illness and of effeminacy (cf. Cicero *On the Response of the Haruspices* 44; Quintilian 11.3.144), categories that overlap in Latin anyway. In another version of the Polemo story, however, it is Polemo's effeminate party clothes that are described at length (Valerius Maximus 6.9.ext.1, first century CE). Indeed, the wording of this letter bears a resemblance to the wording of the passage in Valerius—and Valerius describes Polemo as "dressed in a see-through garment." Haines glosses Polemo as "a tipsy gallant" and translates the accessories as "scarf, spats, lappet"; a 1909 school text of Horace calls Polemo "a young clubman" (Morris 1909 ad loc.). In Fronto's letter, the anecdote perhaps most strongly recalls the images of effeminacy in oratory that Fronto has used in the previous section. Immediately after the bit about Polemo, Horace turns a lover's speech from a play by Terence from dramatic meter into satiric; Fronto is boasting to Marcus that he has done the same thing by turning Horace's poem into a speech. Fronto at once goes on to talk about Marcus's poetry, which Marcus has been writing (as also in letter 19) when, as Fronto has just strongly hinted, he should really be getting on with his rhetorical training by writing prose.

24. Victorinus: See n. 1 above.

25. thread: Fronto here takes unusual precautions; letters are often said to be sealed, but not sewn up with thread. This was a papyrus letter (*chartam,* "page"), which would be rolled up into a cylinder.

26. get into any cracks or crevices: Lat. *rimari,* appropriate for a mouse.

27. hexameters: Dactylic hexameter was the meter of epic and didactic poetry and of satire.

28. your birthday: April 26. The upset on Marcus's birthday does not appear in the letters.

29. If . . . *honi* . . . *pense*!: Lit. "If there's anything bad [going on] for you, '[may

it be] on the head of the Pyrrhaians'!" This whole sentence is in Greek in the original. According to a late ancient proverb collector, the Pyrrhaians were inhabitants of a town on Lesbos much disliked by their neighbors, hence this saying.

30. in you I trust: Fronto here calls Marcus *mea securitas hilaritas gloria,* "my security happiness glory." The Latin word *securitas,* lit. "freedom from care," was used to translate the *ataraxia* of the Epicurean philosophers, and may constitute gentle teasing in the context of Marcus's devotion to the Stoics. It also appears as a slogan on coins in the early years of Antoninus Pius's reign, although not on coins on which Marcus appears (see Mattingly 1940, 179, 209, 216, 220, 276, 285). But *hilaritas* was a slogan on coins that do feature Marcus in these years (Mattingly 1940, xlii), and Fronto seems here to be making a joke based on coin slogans, although *gloria* is so used in no extant example. Mattingly (1940, lxxxii) suggests that the slogan and personified image of *Securitas* on coins of this period may indicate anxiety over various crises and a desire to soothe the fears of the public, although he sees the ideology of Antonine coins as generally denoting dynastic security and public prosperity.

31. shameless: See n. 12 above.

32. barbarism: In the original, *barbarismus,* a Latinized Greek word. It refers to non-Greek speech, which to Greeks sounded like "bar, bar, bar."

33. a hillbilly: Lat. *opicum.* This word originally meant "Oscan" and is a complicated ethnic slur. The Oscans spoke their own language and lived in southern Italy, where their Greek-speaking neighbors sneered at them for not being able to speak Greek; so Gk. *Opikos* = "barbarous" (see n. 32 above). The word then came to mean "ignorant of Latin," i.e., "illiterate." Its use here is, then, somewhat ironic (not that Fronto really means he is ignorant of Greek in any case) and is picked up by Marcus in letter 25. *Opicus* will later be used by Sidonius Apollinaris, in similarly ironic circumstances, to describe his own writing (*Letters* 8.3.1). *Opicus* always has class/ethnic overtones; in English, *boor, churl, slave,* and possibly *nitwit* have similar etymologies, although the class and ethnic atrocities from which they stem have been forgotten. Haines translates "goth."

34. a big kiss: Lat. *savium,* which also means a French kiss or an erotically charged one (see the volume introduction).

Letter 21

To the mother of Caesar,[1]

How shall I defend myself and find forgiveness with you, when I haven't written you these past few days? Or is it obvious that I would if I state the true reason I've had no time? After all, I was getting together a speech about the Great King.[2] The Roman[3] proverb says we must "not hate, but understand, the ways of a friend." And what my way may be I'll tell you, and not hide it. Due to my great lack of talent and my worthlessness,[4] my condition is like that of the creature the Romans call the hyena,[5] whose neck, they say, stretches out straight ahead but cannot be bent to one side or the other. And I, whenever I'm mustering something up especially enthusiastically, am an unbending sort of person, and neglecting everything else I throw myself at that one thing, unstoppably, like the hyena. And they say the snakes called "javelins"[6] shoot forward the same way, straight ahead, and never twist or turn; and spears and arrows most often find their mark whenever they shoot straight and aren't pushed aside by the wind or deflected by the hand of Athena or Apollo, like the ones shot by Teucer or by the suitors.[7]

I've assimilated these three similes[8] to myself, two savage and animal (the ones about the hyena and the snakes), the third one about the projectiles, which is also uncouth[9] and rough.[10] And if I should say that of all the winds a following wind is the one most praised because it bears the ship straight ahead and doesn't let it veer off to the side, this would be the fourth simile and another violent one. And if I should also add the example of a line and say that the most venerable line is the straight line, I would be making a fifth simile, one that's not only inanimate, like the one about the spears, but even incorporeal.[11]

So what simile might be found persuasive? Best of all would be a human one; even better if it were also artistic;[12] and again if it were associated with friendship[13] or passion,[14] the simile would be even more similar. They say that Orpheus[15] howled[16] because he turned back; but if he'd looked straight ahead and kept walking, he wouldn't have howled. Enough similes. I'm sure this simile with Orpheus is a bit unpersuasive, hauled up from Hades the way it is.

So I'll defend myself now the way I might find forgiveness most easily. And what might that be? That in composing the encomium of the King, first of all, I was doing what's most gratifying to you and your son; then that I remembered you and spoke your names in my composition, just as lovers[17] speak the names of their dearest[18] with every cup.[19] But look how my simile mastercraftsmanship[20] is trickling in and sprouting up here. One more has popped up anyway, which I'll add on to all the others, and this one might most appropriately be called a simile or likeness since it's from a painter:[21] they say that the painter Protogenes was painting his *Ialysos*[22] for eleven years, and that he painted nothing else in those eleven years *but* the *Ialysos*. But I was painting not one but two *Ialysos*es at the same time, and not only the two faces, not only the two figures, but the two characters and the two sets of virtues were no medium-sized ones, either of them, or easy to paint, but the one is the Great King who rules the whole earth and sea, the other is the son of the Great King, and is his child in the same way as Athena is the child of Zeus,[23] or, since he's your son, as Hephaistos is the son of Hera[24]—though let's forget the question of feet in this simile with Hephaistos. So my self-defense, then, is turning out to be a totally similitudinous and painterly one, overflowing with similes and then some.

Still, as they do in geometry, I'll ask—but what?[25] If any of the words in this letter should be unauthorized or barbaric[26] or otherwise illegitimate or not totally Attic,[27] I hereby request that you disregard it, but consider the word's meaning in itself; for you know I'm interested in words and diction for their own sake. And after all they say that famous Scythian, Anacharsis,[28] didn't speak totally Attic Greek, but he was praised for his meaning and his thoughts. Not that I would compare myself with Anacharsis for wisdom, good heavens, but for being a barbarian like him. After all, he was a Scythian of the nomad Scythians, I am a Libyan of the Libyan nomads.[29] So it's common to both of us, Anacharsis and me, to be driven to pasture; and it will be our common deed to baa[30] when we are grazing as best anyone can baa. Well, now I've made a simile between talking like a barbarian and baaing. So I'll stop, since I can write nothing but similes.

Notes

1. To . . . Caesar: This letter is written in Greek, specifically in the classicizing Attic Greek much in style during this period (see n. 3, letter 3). Like Fronto's other writing, it contains some made-up words; it somewhat excessively demonstrates what he can do with similes. Some have found Fronto's Greek style here lacking; the letter is certainly stilted. One other letter from Fronto to Marcus's mother, Domitia Lucilla, is extant in the collection, and it is also in Greek: birthday wishes, tied to a visit of Cratia's (see letter 26). It seems possible that Herodes Atticus's childhood stay in Domitia Lucilla's father's house (letter 8) indicates a general family interest in Greek culture. None of Domitia Lucilla's letters in reply, if there were any, are preserved; as in the collection of Pliny's letters, responses from women are lacking, although Pliny's collection does preserve replies from some of his addressees (notably the emperor Trajan). Cicero is known to have written to a learned woman named Caerellia, and a whole book of his letters to his wife is extant in his letter collection, but none of their replies are preserved among the many letters replying to Cicero. It is a remarkable fact that, although Roman women seem to have shared in the intellectual world of these letter writers and to have had their respect, what women wrote was just discarded.

2. the Great King: The emperor, Antoninus Pius. This locution is reserved in Herodotus for the king of Persia. Greeks used the word "king" to refer to the emperor as early as the reign of Augustus (*Greek Anthology* 10.25.5), but not usually "Great King"; Holford-Strevens (1988, 6) points out that resistance to the king of Persia was a chief claim of the classical Athens so admired by Fronto's contemporaries. The speech is probably the one referred to by Marcus in letter 23.

3. Roman: Here, to match the language of his letter, Fronto adopts the pose of a Greek writing about the Romans as an outsider; this is given an entertaining twist as it becomes clear that Fronto is writing as an African.

4. my . . . worthlessness: For this pose of modesty and unworthiness, see the beginning of letter 2. The word translated "worthlessness," Gk. *outheneias* (lit. "nothingness"), is used by Socrates when he tells Phaedrus he cannot understand some things about Lysias's *erôtikos logos* (*Phaedrus* 235a).

5. hyena: A striking analogy and one packed with meanings, some very odd. Ovid's *Metamorphoses* (15.409–10) includes a graphically sexual depiction of hyena serial androgyny (each hyena switches back and forth from male to female). Hyenas are again androgynous in Pliny's *Natural History* (8.105–6), where their necks

are said not to bend—Fronto's expressed point here. Hyenas are said to come from Africa, although not specifically from Libya, and their traits include, besides eating carrion, digging up graves; their body parts are said to be useful for various unsavory medical needs, both by Pliny (who lists over seventy uses) and other medical writers and by Lucan, who puts hyena parts into a witch's brew. They are only rarely mentioned as appearing in the arena—and not until 248 CE (*HA Life of the Three Gordians* 33.1). For the wide diffusion of the idea of the hyena's androgyny in antiquity and its increasingly common association with male homoeroticism in late antiquity and the Middle Ages, see Boswell 1980, 138–43, 316–18, 356–58. The pose of two hyenas embracing in a twelfth-century manuscript margin (Boswell 1980, pl. 9) looks just like vase paintings of Greek pederastic intercourse.

6. snakes called "javelins": Gk. *akontia*. Snakes called *iaculi* in Latin (rel. Lat. *iaculum*, "javelin") figure in the great catalog of scary snakes in the younger Cato's march through the Libyan desert in Lucan's epic poem *On the Civil War* (*iaculi* at 9.720, 9.823; cf. Pliny *Natural History* 8.85). They supposedly launched themselves from trees straight at their prey.

7. Teucer . . . suitors: Two Homeric references. Teucer was the half brother of the great Greek hero Ajax and a famous archer; at *Iliad* 8.311 he tries to shoot the Trojan hero Hector, but his arrow is turned aside by Apollo. He is the son of a Greek king and a captive Asian woman and stands inferior to Ajax as both weaker and of hybrid birth. The suitors were those of Penelope in the *Odyssey*, who are shot by Odysseus on his return with the assistance of his patron, Athena.

8. similes: Gk. *eikonas*, "likenesses," from the root that means "like." Fronto plays with the cognates of this word throughout the letter; on *eoikas*, see n. 8, letter 2. On similes, see letters 4, 32, and 44.

9. uncouth: Gk. *apanthrôpon*, used of places that are far from man, wild, unsocial.

10. rough: Gk. *amouson*, "without the Muses, rude, uncultivated." The picture that Fronto is building up of himself ties him to Africa, hunting, the desert, things threatening and hostile, and particularly the use of weapons; he is the Wild Man. This is somewhat ironic since, in the letters, it is Marcus who goes hunting. Fronto speaks of hunting only once, and this is to ask Marcus to be careful, although he may be speaking from experience (see letter 36). So it is a figurative wildness. It's also markedly linear and thrusting.

11. incorporeal: Van den Hout (1999, 58) points out that Fronto has here been ringing the changes on the varieties of simile as prescribed by ancient rhetorical theory.

12. artistic: Gk. *mousikê*, "of the Muses."

13. friendship: Gk. *philia*.

14. passion: Gk. *erôtos*.

15. Orpheus: The great poet of Greek mythology, who tried to get his beloved Eurydice back from the underworld (she'd died of snakebite). His songs moved Hades to let her go, on the condition that Orpheus not look back until he and Eurydice reached the upper world. He failed, and she was lost. The story was told by Vergil in the *Georgics,* and Ovid makes Orpheus the narrator of the tenth book of the *Metamorphoses.* After Eurydice's death, Orpheus abandoned women for boys; see letter 11, where Fronto uses Orpheus as a figure for Marcus.

16. howled: Gk. *oimôxai,* lit. "say *oimoi,*" the Greek cry of lament at funerals. It was a wail or howl; perhaps here it is invoked in order to echo the hyena simile?

17. lovers: Gk. *erastai.* See n. 9, letter 2, and the volume introduction.

18. dearest: Gk. *philtatous.*

19. with every cup: This custom is attested, e.g., in the epigrams of the *Greek Anthology,* as a sort of toast (although the beloved need not be present). It certainly belongs to the world of *erôs* and not of friendship; it is odd to find Marcus's mother here along with him. See nn. 6 and 10 to letter 34, from Fronto to Herodes Atticus.

20. mastercraftsmanship: Gk. *technôsis,* evidently a coinage of Fronto's.

21. most . . . a painter: See n. 8 above on Gr. *eikôn,* "simile/likeness." Painting is commonly likened to rhetoric (e.g., Quintilian 12.10.1–10); see letter 23, where Fronto is compared with great artists.

22. Protogenes . . . *Ialysos:* Protogenes was a famous painter of the late fourth century BCE, a rival of Apelles; the *Ialysos,* now lost, was his masterpiece. Ialysos was a mythical local hero of Rhodes; the elder Pliny says that the painting was in the temple of Pax in Rome (*Natural History* 35.102–5) and that the special touch of mastery in the painting was the foam in the mouth of Ialysos's dog. Moreover, says Pliny, King Demetrius the Besieger held off from burning Rhodes just to save this picture, paying a special visit to Protogenes to admire his work and allowing Protogenes to sass him.

23. Athena, Zeus: An instance of a great child sprung from a great father. Athena was born from Zeus's head, thus bypassing her mother, Metis. So this is not only a transgender example but also, perhaps, a tactless one, a faux pas that Fronto goes on to compound (see n. 24 below).

24. Hephaistos, Hera: Having already given a tactless example (see n. 23 above), Fronto goes on to one even more tactless. Hephaistos was the son of Hera, queen of the gods, without any father; in addition, he was lame (although powerful) and a laughingstock to the other gods (cf. n. 10, letter 33, on Fronto's use of Philoctetes). In some stories, Hera throws him out of Olympus when she sees he is lame. Hephaistos is closely associated with Athena in several myths, in one of which he tries to rape her. Fronto here may be dealing partly with the fact

that Antoninus Pius was Marcus's adoptive father and had a wife of his own; Domitia Lucilla's husband, Marcus's father, had died in Marcus's childhood.

25. geometry . . . but what?: Presumably this refers to the *QED* at the end of a proof in geometry.

26. barbaric: Gk. *barbaron*. It was a quintessentially Greek idea that all peoples but the Greeks sounded as if they were speaking gibberish ("bar, bar"). Fronto's beloved Plautus adopted *barbarus,* the Latin version of the Greek *barbaros,* with irony, to mean "Roman" in his plays, thus speaking as insider and outsider simultaneously; Fronto here does something similar, as he does elsewhere with the words *barbarismus* and *opicus* (see, respectively, nn. 32 and 33, letter 20).

27. not totally Attic: See n. 3, letter 3.

28. Anacharsis: A legendary Scythian prince (sixth century BCE), famous for his critique of Greek customs, a sort of noble savage. Scythians were known as horse nomads and archers, and Scythia (roughly, Russia), like Fronto's native Libya, was considered savage, barbaric, exotic, far away, hence the surprisingness of Anacharsis's wisdom.

29. I . . . nomads: A famous line, the one place where Fronto explicitly raises the question of his ethnicity. (On Fronto's background, see the volume introduction.) The claim to nomad status does not seem to be meant literally here, but it does form part of Fronto's self-portrait in this letter as a rough, tough straight shooter and wild man. The whole letter seems (similes must be contagious) much like the displays of animals who puff themselves up in order to frighten off attackers; its ostensible message is very small for such an elaborate essay ("sorry I haven't written, I've been busy"), and Fronto tells Domitia Lucilla outright to read between the lines, so we might expect this huge mass of similes to contain another message. It doesn't seem to be a friendly message, either.

30. baa: Fronto's last simile for himself shifts abruptly from wolf to sheep, evidently taking off from himself and Anacharsis as nomads (herdsmen).

Letter 22

<Marcus Caesar to his most magnificent consul Fronto>,
   . . . [several pages lost between previous letter in manuscript and this one] allied by relation through marriage, and not placed under guardianship,[1] and what's more, set in that lot in life in which, as Quintus Ennius[2] says, "Everyone gives counsel pointless, and for pleasure, everything"—the same way that Plautus says outstandingly in the *Flatterer*[3] about the same thing:

Men who took a solemn oath and then tricked one who trusted them,
underhanded under-yesmen, who are nearest to a king,
who say one thing to the king in words but have another in their head.

Of course once upon a time these nuisances used to affect kings only, but of course now there's no shortage of men "who even with the sons of kings," as Naevius[4] says, "would guard their tongues[5] and nod their heads and act like slaves." So it's no wonder, my teacher, I burn so; no wonder I've appointed one man of mine as my *veilleur;*[6] no wonder I think of one person when the pen comes to my hand.[7]
   You ask for my hexameters[8] in the most delightful way, and I would have sent them, too, on the double, if I had them with me. In fact my secretary—you know him, I mean Anicetus[9]—when I was setting out, he sent none of my writings with me. Of course he knows my sickness and he was afraid that, if they had gotten into my grasp, I would do what I usually do and dispatch them into the stove. But really there was practically no danger for those old[10] hexameters. If I can confess the truth to my teacher, I love them. Here I work at night, because in the daytime our time is used up at the theater. So I do less in the evenings, because I'm tired, and I get up in the morning still sleeping. Still I've made excerpts for myself these past few days out of sixty books, five pages full.[11] But when

you read "sixty," that includes the Novian mini-farces[12] and the mini-speeches[13] of Scipio[14]—don't get too shook up at the number.

Since you reminded me of your Polemo, I ask you, don't remind me of Horace, who as far as I'm concerned is dead and gone along with Polio.[15] Good-bye my dearest[16] one, good-bye my most loving one, consul most magnificent, sweetest teacher, whom I haven't seen for two years now. After all, when people say it's been two months, they only count the days. Will it be when I see you?[17]

Notes

1. guardianship: Lat. *tutelae,* a legal term for the guardianship of children *sui iuris* (without a *paterfamilias*) and under the age of puberty (for which the standard age, for males, was fourteen). See Crook 1967, 113–16.

2. Quintus Ennius: See n. 3, letter 12. This line exhibits Ennius's usual taste for alliteration and repetition; it comes from an otherwise unknown tragedy or comedy. The translation reproduces the meter of the original.

3. *Flatterer:* Gk. *Colax.* This comedy is lost; for Plautus, see n. 5, letter 17. The translation reproduces the meter of the original.

4. Naevius: See n. 7, letter 17. Another fragment of a lost comedy or tragedy; this one, like others in Marcus's letters, is slightly off, a line of verse missing a word or two.

5. guard their tongues: Lat. *linguis faveant,* "favor their tongues," a phrase used of the observation of religious silence to avoid words of ill omen.

6. one . . . *veilleur:* Mixed Lat./Gk. *unum meum skopon,* "one man as guard/lookout"; *skopon* is in Greek letters in the text. Both Haines and van den Hout (1999, 72) here take *skopon* in the sense "target/goal/aim," in which case this clause would mean "I have set up this one *objectif* of mine for myself," implying that Fronto would understand what that was; Fronto employs this sense when he writes to Marcus's mother in letter 21 of always hitting his *skopos*. But all three of these clauses must be about Fronto—and about him as trustworthy in a way that Marcus's courtiers are not.

7. when the pen . . . hand: For Marcus's pen fetish, see letter 18. On the letters as written by hand, see also letters 9, 12, 32, 33, 40, and 41.

8. hexameters: See n. 27, letter 20.

9. Anicetus: A Greek name that literally means "unconquered." This is, ironically, a slave name, although it may be the man's birth name.

10. those old: Lat. *istis.* This demonstrative pronoun often indicates contempt or dismissiveness, as here (see the volume introduction).

11. five pages full: Lit. "in five *tomi*"; a *tomus* was a length of papyrus. For the custom of making excerpts from reading, see letter 13.

12. Novian mini-farces: Lat. *Novianae atellaniolae,* "Novian Atellanettes." Novius (early first century BCE) was one of the most famous writers of Atellan farces; originally these plays were an oral tradition of coarse, short sketches, set in the small towns of Italy, featuring three or four stock low-life characters a lot like the Three Stooges. Marcus and Fronto love early Roman comedy for its inventive vocabulary; see, e.g., *under-yesmen* in the Plautus excerpt in this letter. And, in fact, Marcus here makes up the diminutive *atellaniolae.*

13. mini-speeches: Lat. *oratiunculae.* As with *Novianae atellaniolae* (see n. 12 above), the diminutive here seems to mean that the speeches are short. The word *oratiunculae* was not coined by Marcus but is used by Cicero both in his letters and in his other writings as well as by other letter writers (the younger Pliny, Symmachus) and by other writers on rhetoric (Quintilian, Tacitus). The diminutive ending still must give it a somewhat colloquial tone.

14. Scipio: Probably Publius Cornelius Scipio Aemilianus, the great soldier and literary patron of the mid-first century BCE.

15. Polemo . . . Horace . . . Polio: See letters 19 and 20. It would be reasonable to assume that *Polione* here is a manuscript error for *Polemone,* the Greek philosopher Fronto wrote about in letter 20. This would then mean "Horace is as dead and gone as Polemo"—who had been dead for over four hundred years. If *Polione* is right, Marcus means either Asinius Pollio, another Augustan writer, whom Fronto perhaps discusses in a later letter to Marcus's brother Verus (Haines 2.142–43 = *Ad Verum* 2.1= van den Hout, p. 125, line 24, but the text is corrupt), or (doubtfully) a teacher of his in former years who may have been named Polio (*HA Life of Marcus* 2.3).

16. dearest: Lat. *amicissime.*

17. Will it be when I see you?: This is literally what the Latin says: *eritne quom te videbo.* Haines translates "Shall I ever see you?" and van den Hout (1999, 75) provides only a brief comment on *est cum* as the equivalent of *est tempus cum,* "there is (a) time when" (so *eritne quom* would mean "will there be a time when . . . ?"). It seems possible that Marcus here speaks elliptically, referring to something not spelled out in the letter.

Letter 23

\<Marcus Caesar to his consul and teacher\>,

All right, if the ancient Greeks wrote anything that good, let the experts sort it out; but if it's legal to say so, I never noticed Marcus Porcius[1] giving out insults as well as you were giving out praise.[2] Oh if my Lord[3] could be praised adequately, you were definitely the one to do it! *Si la jeunesse pouvait . . .*[4] A person could imitate Phidias[5] more easily, Apelles[6] more easily, even Demosthenes[7] himself more easily, or Cato himself, than this work, so perfect and polished. I have never read anything more elegant, more old-world,[8] more well-seasoned, more Latin. Oh what a lucky person you are to be so gifted in rhetoric! Oh what a lucky person I am to be given to this teacher! Oh the decor![9] Oh the vogue![10] Oh the elegance! Oh the charm! Oh the grace! Oh the words! Oh the brilliance! Oh the cleverness! Oh the élan![11] Oh the chic![12] Oh everything![13] I'll die,[14] if someday the scepter[15] isn't going to be placed in your hand, the tiara set on your head, the judge's bench set up for you:[16] then the announcer should call us all out—why am I saying "us"? I mean all the professors and accomplished speakers like that—and you should point to each one of them with your scepter and caution them with your words. I have no fear of such a caution as yet; much yet remains to be done before I set foot in your school.[17]

I'm writing all this to you with the greatest haste, because when I was sending on such a kind letter to you from my Lord, what did I need with longer letters? And so good-bye, you jewel of Roman rhetoric, your friends' pride and joy, *el grande,*[18] you most delightful person, most magnificent consul, sweetest teacher.

From now on you'd better watch out and not tell so many lies about me, especially in the senate. The way you wrote that speech is awesome![19] Oh if I could kiss your head at every heading of it! *Touché!*[20] Now that I've read that speech I know it's a waste for us to study, a waste for us to work, a waste for us to strain our muscles. Be well always, sweetest teacher.

Notes

1. Marcus Porcius: The elder Cato (see n. 6, letter 7; and letters 18, 19, and 20). The tone is slightly familiar, like "Percy Bysshe" or "Ralph Waldo" for Shelley or Emerson.

2. praise: The circumstances of this letter seem to be that Fronto has given his big speech thanking the emperor (August 13, 143 CE) and has sent a copy to the emperor and Marcus; Marcus responds.

3. my Lord: The emperor, Antoninus Pius.

4. *Si . . . pouvait . . .* : "If the young could only . . ."; this line is in Greek in the original, and literally says, "This kind of deed doesn't happen these days."

5. Phidias: The famous Greek sculptor (fifth century BCE); think "Michelangelo."

6. Apelles: The famous Greek painter (fourth century BCE); think "Leonardo."

7. Demosthenes: Known as the greatest Greek orator (fourth century BCE); think "Machiavelli."

8. more old-world: Lat. *antiquius.* Fronto was one of the chief advocates of an elaborate style that used a lot of old vocabulary—hence the fondness of Marcus and Fronto for early Latin writers (cf. letters 20 and 33). Compare the late Victorian fondness for medieval and Renaissance style.

9. decor: Gk. *epicheirêmata,* lit. "undertaking"; as a rhetorical technical term, an argument based on an example.

10. vogue: Gk. *taxis,* lit. "arrangement"; as a rhetorical technical term, the proper organization of a speech.

11. élan: This word, *kharites,* appears in the manuscript in the Roman alphabet, but it is a Greek word meaning "graces."

12. chic: Gk. *askêsis,* lit. "exercise" or "art"; as a rhetorical term, "skill." This word came to stand for a major range of bodily and intellectual practices during this period (see Foucault 1988; Perkins 1995).

13. everything: Van den Hout (1999, 68) quips that Marcus's string of twelve exclamations holds the record in Latin prose.

14. I'll die: Lit. "May I not be well"; a colloquial oath, attesting the truth of what follows.

15. scepter: Lat. *virga,* "wand, rod of office."

16. scepter . . . you: Marcus seems to be imagining a sort of courtroom or throne room of rhetoric; the *tribunal* (judge's bench) was an official dais for Roman magistrates (see letter 17, where Fronto has one as consul), but a *diadema* (here translated *tiara*) to a Roman was something foreign, Asian, effeminate, suspicious, and non-Roman, and this is a very odd combination. The beauty-contest tone of the translation echoes the tone of the Latin.

17. school: Lat. *ludus.* Here Marcus seems to change the metaphor again. A *ludus* was an elementary school; *ludus* was also the word for a gladiatorial troupe and for a public spectacle, and it seems possible that what Marcus has in mind here is a display at the Circus, with Fronto as emperor deciding the fate of the other rhetoricians, below him in the arena. Heralds (*praecones*) were the official announcers at various kinds of public *ludi,* and announced the victors at *ludi* involving contests.

18. *el grande:* Gk. *mega pragma,* "big thing," "big deal," "big business."

19. awesome: Lat. *horribiliter,* "horribly." This must be slang and is first seen in Latin here. Marcus also likes the word *vehementer,* "violently," which also seems to be slang for him and is here translated *terribly* or *awfully.*

20. *Touché*!: Lit. "You've totally put them all to scorn." This is in Greek in the original.

Letter 24

The consul to his Caesar,

My lucky brother,[1] to have seen you for those two whole days! But I'm stuck in Rome, bound by my golden shackles, and I don't look forward to the first of September any differently than those religious fanatics[2] look forward to the star that lets them break[3] their fast once they've seen it. Good-bye, Caesar, jewel of the fatherland and of the Roman name. Good-bye, Lord.

Notes

1. brother: For Fronto's brother, see n. 6, letter 12.

2. religious fanatics: Lat. *superstitiosi;* Fronto means the Jews, whose religion was regarded by mainstream Romans as bizarre. This comparison places Fronto in an abject position—cf. letters 11, 20, 21, 41, 44, and 45—compensated for by the "golden shackles" of his consulship. Shackles were worn primarily by slaves. And note the analogy between Marcus and food (cf. n. 3, letter 26).

3. break: Fronto uses the word *polluant,* "defile" (see n. 8, letter 9). This phrase is found elsewhere and may be an idiom.

Letter 25

Marcus Aurelius Caesar to his consul and teacher, hello.

After I wrote you most recently, afterward—nothing worthwhile to write you about or that would be any pleasure to you to know about. In fact we've passed the days practically *de même*[1]— the same theater, the same boredom,[2] the same longing for you. Why am I saying "the same"? No, every day it's renewed and swells; and as Laberius[3] says of love, in his own way and à la his own inimitable style,[4] "Your love grows as quick as a leek, as firm as a palm tree."[5] I'm applying this then to longing, what he says about love. I want to write you more, but nothing suggests itself.

Look what comes to mind. We were listening to some panegyricists[6] here, Greeks, naturally, but amazing creatures, so that I, who am as far off Greek literature as my old Caelian Hill[7] is from the land of Greece, was still hoping that in comparison with them I could even equal Theopompus[8]—he's the one, after all, I hear was born the most accomplished speaker among the Greeks. So persons, as Caecilius[9] says, of "unendangered ignorance" have inspired me—practically a hillbilly[10]—and given me a shove toward writing in Greek.

The weather[11] in Naples[12] is all right, but awfully changeable. Every milligram[13] of an hour it gets colder or warmer or more scorching.[14] At first the night will be warm, like at Laurentum; but then at cockcrow it's chilly, like at Lanuvium; now in the quiet hour and dawn and half-light[15] until sunrise it's cold, as bad as it gets at Algidus; after that the morning is sunny, like at Tusculum; then at noon it's boiling, like at Puteoli; but when the Sun sets out for his bath in the ocean, finally the weather gets milder, the kind of thing you get at Tibur;[16] and this continues in the same way at evening and when it's time to go to bed at night, when, as Marcus Porcius[17] says, "the dead of night[18] falls headlong." But why am I piling up crazy talk[19] like Masurius[20] when I promised I'd write just a tiny few things?

And so good-bye, kindest teacher, most magnificent consul, and as much as you love me, that's how much you should long for me.

Notes

1. *de même:* Lit. "in the same things." This is in Greek in the original.

2. boredom: Lat. *odium,* also "hatefulness." Variant readings are *odeum,* "music hall," and *otium,* "nothing to do."

3. Laberius: Roman comic playwright (first century BCE). This is another loose quotation from a work now lost (again, the meter is off; see n. 4, letter 22).

4. à la his own inimitable style: Gk. *kai epi idiai mousai,* "and according to his own Muse."

5. leek . . . palm tree: These somewhat suggestive images might be compared with Marcus's word choice in letter 28.

6. panegyricists: Lat. *encomiagraphos,* a Latinized Greek word (appearing only here) meaning "writers of formal praises." A panegyric written by the younger Pliny for the emperor Trajan is extant; cf. the speech in praise of Antoninus Pius that Fronto made in the senate, discussed in letters 17, 21, and 23.

7. Caelian Hill: One of the seven hills of Rome. Marcus was born there and lived there as a child (*HA Life of Marcus* 1.5).

8. Theopompus: A historian and orator of the fourth century BCE. His histories were famous for their use of rhetoric, and Marcus's remark here may be picking up on something Fronto has said, possibly in an assignment.

9. Caecilius: Caecilius Statius, Roman comic playwright (second century BCE).

10. hillbilly: Lat. *opicum.* On Fronto's use of this word in a similar situation, see n. 33, letter 20; Marcus of course does not really mean that he is bad at Greek, either.

11. weather: Marcus really must be bored; this is the only place in the correspondence of these years where either Marcus or Fronto falls back on the weather as a topic. Or is what follows a sort of list of mementos?

12. Naples: The Bay of Naples was a major Roman resort area; several of Marcus's letters are written from there (cf. the discussion of Baiae in letter 15, nn. 6 and 7).

13. milligram: Lat. *scripulis;* a *scripula* was 1/288 of anything, usually in weight. This is the only place in Latin where it is used of time.

14. more scorching: Lat. *torridius.* The text may have said *horridius,* "rougher."

15. half-light: Marcus, showing off, here strings together a list of country terms for phases of the night, some of which are rarely attested. Each seems to move a bit closer to sunrise, and the overall effect is of someone with insomnia watching the clock.

16. Tibur: The places named in this passage are all upscale towns in Italy, full of villas of the rich and famous. Hadrian had a villa at Tibur; Cicero had one at Tusculum, which was also the birthplace of Marcus's beloved Cato.

17. Marcus Porcius: Cato (see n. 6, letter 7, and n. 1, letter 23).

18. dead of night: Lat. *intempesta nox,* lit. "stormy night" or "unseasonable night," but commonly used in this sense.

19. crazy talk: Lat. *deliramenta,* a Plautine word used again by Laberius (in a line quoted by Fronto in letter 33) and also picked up by Fronto's contemporary Apuleius.

20. like Masurius: This evidently refers to the famous law professor Masurius Sabinus (early first century CE); he was known for long-winded detail and wrote a standard textbook (think "Blackstone"). Marcus, who often says how boring he finds it to listen to lawyers and who must have had to read law as well as rhetoric, must be accusing himself of going on about a boring subject, which, indeed, he is, or seems to be.

Letter 26

To my Lord,

I've sent my Cratia[1] to celebrate your mother's birthday[2] with her and I've told her to stay there until I arrive. After all, at the very same instant I take my final oath as consul I'm getting in my wagon and flying to you all. Meanwhile I've given my Cratia my word that there'll be no danger of starvation: of course your mother's going to share the tidbits[3] you send her with her client lady.[4] And my Cratia isn't a big eater, either, the way people say lawyers'[5] wives are. She could live on your mother's kisses alone and be happy. But then what'll happen to me? There's not even a single kiss left anywhere at Rome. All my fortunes, all my joys are at Naples.

I ask you, what is with this custom of being sworn out of office a day early? What if I'm ready to swear by more gods if I could swear my resignation oath more days previously? And what is this thing where I have to swear that I'm leaving the consulship? Truly, I'll even swear that I've long since wanted to quit the consulship so that I could put my arms around Marcus Aurelius.[6]

Notes

1. Cratia: Fronto's wife.

2. birthday: One of the few extant letters written by a Roman woman invites another to a birthday party (Bowman 1994, 127). On women and letter writing, see n. 1, letter 21.

3. tidbits: Lat. *particulas.* Probably meant figuratively, of emotional nourishment, although van den Hout glosses "perhaps fancy pastry" (1999, 86): translate "goodies"? For Marcus as food, see n. 2, letter 24.

4. client lady: Lat. *clienta,* a word Fronto dredges up out of Plautus, where it is used for women of very low status; it is a feminine form of the word *cliens* (see n. 2, letter 15). We know very little about how patronage worked for Roman women, if it did at all.

5. lawyers': Fronto uses the somewhat pejorative term *causidicorum;* a *causidicus* was someone who made a living by arguing cases in court for a fee, lowly by comparison with a grand orator, politician, and attorney like Fronto (who,

like all senators, would be required by law to take no pay). The word *causidicus* literally means "case-pleader," and the tone verges on "ambulance-chaser." See van den Hout 1999, 86–87. Marcus uses the word himself in a pejorative sense in letters 30 and 38; cf. n. 20, letter 25.

6. I've long since wanted . . . Marcus Aurelius: This is a very remarkable passage. The consulship was the pinnacle of Fronto's career. Although by this time the consulship itself would have been a mostly ceremonial position, and Fronto held only a suffect consulship, lasting for two months, still it was a crowning honor, especially for a man from the provinces. Note that, while Fronto holds a suffect consulship for 143, his nemesis Herodes Atticus was *consul ordinarius* for the year—one of the two consuls by whose names the year would be designated. It is not possible to imagine Cicero writing such a thing—or even the uxorious younger Pliny. Compare letter 33.

Letter 27

MARCUS TO FRONTO, ? EARLY SEPTEMBER, 143 CE

To my teacher,

Cratia Junior[1] finished what Cratia Senior[2] started—she either lowers our anxiety level[3] in the meantime or actually wipes it away altogether. I thank you on behalf of my mentor Marcus Porcius[4] because you keep reading him frequently; I'm afraid you'll never be able to thank me on behalf of Gaius Crispus,[5] because I've dedicated and also devoted and also delivered myself to Marcus Porcius alone. And where do you think this "and also" itself comes from? From my craze.[6] The day after tomorrow will be a red-letter day for me if you're definitely coming. Good-bye, my lovingest and rarest person, sweetest teacher.

On the day of this senate meeting it seems more like we'll be here than go there. But either way it's up in the air. You just come the day after tomorrow, and who cares what happens. Always be well for me, my soul; my mother says hello to you and your family.

Notes

1. Cratia Junior: Fronto's young daughter, named after her mother. She was the only one of Fronto's six children to survive infancy.

2. Cratia Senior: Fronto's wife.

3. anxiety level: Fronto seems to have fallen ill just as he was ending his consulship and getting ready to go see Marcus, although letters 27–31 bear no dates and are not certainly a sequence.

4. Marcus Porcius: The elder Cato, now a favorite author of Marcus's (see n. 6, letter 7).

5. Gaius Crispus: The historian Sallust, another archaizing writer much admired by Marcus and Fronto (see n. 6, letter 7).

6. craze: Lat. *furore.* Cato's style was paratactic—instead of subordinate clauses, he favored strings of independent clauses linked by conjunctions like *and also* (cf. letter 18). He also liked alliteration, as imitated without comment by Marcus here. Both features can be seen in abundance in the writing of the novelist and rhetorician Apuleius, Fronto's contemporary and fellow proponent of the "African style."

Letter 28

To my teacher,

What do you think the state of my soul has been, when I think how long it is that I haven't seen you, and why I haven't seen you! And perhaps for a tiny few days still I won't see you, while you firm yourself up,[1] as you must. So, while you're lying there, my soul will be flat on its back,[2] too; and when, with the gods' help, you stand upright, my soul will stand as well, which is now parched with the most burning longing for you. Be well, soul of your Caesar, your friend, your student.

Notes

1. firm yourself up: Lat. *confirmas,* "grow strong/become steady on your feet/become firm." Letter 25 employs similarly suggestive imagery.

2. flat on its back: Lat. *supinus;* perhaps an echo of Catullus 32.10? If so, this letter is certainly erotic.

Letter 29

To my teacher,

As much as for me you . . .[2] in two days now, if it seems good; still let's grit our teeth; and to make the trip shorter for you because of your recent illness, wait for us at Caieta.[3] I'm acting goofy—what usually happens to people when what they desire is finally at hand: they dither, they overflow, they're jumpy: me, truthfully I'm actually turning my nose up at everything. My lady mother says hello; I'll ask her today to bring Cratia[4] to me—as the Greek poet says, "even the smoke of your fatherland."[5] Be well for me—my everything—my teacher. I love myself because I'm going to see you.

Notes

1. The content of this letter bears a strong resemblance to that of letters 27–28 and 30–31, and it should perhaps be dated around the time they were written; see van den Hout 1999, 191.

2. The first few words of this letter are inferred from a table of contents that remains for this part of the collection, but the actual beginning of the letter was lost with four missing pages of the manuscript; these pages included other letters too, so we cannot know how much is missing between "you" and "in."

3. Caieta: A town on the coast between Rome and Naples.

4. Cratia: Fronto's wife (see letters 26 and 27). She was a friend of Marcus's mother.

5. Greek . . . fatherland: The poet is Homer; the reference is to *Odyssey* 1.58, where Odysseus wishes he could see "even the smoke [i.e., from hearth fires] curling upward" from his homeland, to which he so longed to return—a phrase commonly quoted. So here Cratia is the smoke, Fronto the fatherland (or fire). Marcus quotes this line earlier, in his essay against sleep (Haines 1.94–95 = *M. Caes.* 1.4 = van den Hout, p. 7, line 6).

Letter 30

To my teacher,

You, when you're without me, read Cato,[1] but I, when I'm without you, listen to lawyers[2] until five o'clock. I definitely wish this damn night that's coming would be as short as possible. It'd be worth it to have less time to burn the midnight oil if I could see you sooner. Good-bye my sweetest teacher. My mother says hello. I hardly have breath, I'm so tired.

Notes

1. Cato: See n. 6, letter 7.
2. lawyers: Lat. *causidicos.* See n. 5, letter 26.

Letter 31

To my teacher,

I didn't write you this morning because I'd heard you were more comfortable, and because I was busy myself with some chore; I can't bear to write you anything ever except with a mind that's relaxed and loose and free. So, if we're okay, make sure I know; of course what I want, you know; how deservedly I want it, I know. Be well, my teacher—you deservedly come before everyone in every way in my mind. My teacher, look, I'm not sleepy, and I'm forcing myself to sleep, so you won't get mad at me.[2] Anyway you realize I'm writing this at nightfall.

Notes

1. This letter is not securely dated, but it may form part of the series of letters about Marcus and Fronto's delayed reunion after Fronto's consulship.

2. sleep . . . me: This may refer to an exchange of letters (Haines 1.90–107 = *M. Caes.* 1.4, 1.5, 3.15, 3.16 = van den Hout, pp. 5–9, 47–50), probably from 143 CE, in which Marcus and Fronto debate the merits of sleep within an ongoing and more serious debate on the value of rhetoric (see n. 2, letter 1; n. 3, letter 10; letter 16).

Letter 32

Marcus Aurelius Caesar says hello to Fronto his teacher,

For sure I was shameless[1] ever to give over any of my writings to be read by such genius, such judgment. For my father—my Lord[2]—I even did an adequate job of performing[3] a section of your speech that he had me pick out. They were definitely crying out for their own author to be given back to them: in the end I was hardly greeted with shouts of "*Bravissimo!*"[4] But I won't put off any longer what you deservedly prefer to anything else. My Lord was so affected by what he heard that he just about had a fit because he had to go to work just then someplace else, not where you would be appearing and giving your speech. He was terribly impressed with the command of ideas, the strong range of modes of expression, the clever originality of the arguments, the expert structure of the speech. Now after this I bet you're asking what I liked best. Here it is, then: I began from here:[5]

In those matters and cases that are judged by private judges, there is no danger because their verdicts have validity only within the boundaries of the cases; but from your decisions, Emperor, precedents are publicly enacted that will be valid in perpetuity. So much greater is your force and power than what is allotted to the Fates. The Fates decide what may happen to each of us individually; when you make a decision about individuals, you thereby bind these precedents upon everyone.

Wherefore, if this decision of the proconsul has pleased you, you will have given a model to all the magistrates of all the provinces for what they should decide in cases of this sort. What will happen then? Evidently this: that all the wills from faraway provinces overseas will be referred to you for a hearing. A son suspects he's been disinherited: he'll request that the estate documents of his father not be opened. A daughter will request the same thing, a grandson, a great-great-grandson, a brother, a cousin, a father's brother, a mother's brother, a father's sister, a mother's sister; all the degrees of relationship will encroach on this privilege, just so they can forbid the documents to be opened and enjoy possession by right of blood. And what will happen in the end, when the case has been referred to Rome? The stipulated heirs will set sail, while the disinherited remain in possession, dragging on day after day, looking for postponements and putting off the hearings with all kinds of excuses. It's winter, and the sea is rough in winter; he couldn't get here. When winter's gone by, now it's the winds of spring, uncertain and fickle, that have been causing delays. Spring is over? It's hot in summer! The sun could burn a voyager! A person could get seasick! Autumn comes next: now it's the crops' fault, he's tired, that's his excuse.

Am I making this up? Am I writing fiction?[6] What, didn't the same thing happen in this very case? Where is the opposing party who should have been here long ago to plead his case? "He's on the way." At what point on the way, then? "He's coming from Asia."[7] And is he still in Asia? "It's a long journey even when they're hurrying." Is it by ship, on horseback, or by imperial mail that he's making such lightning-speed layovers? Meanwhile, Caesar, when the hearing is announced by you for the first time, a stay is requested and granted; the second time it's announced, for a second time a stay of two months is requested. Two months were over on the last Ides, and several more of those pesky days have gone by since then. Is he here yet? If he isn't here yet, surely at least he's almost here? If he's not almost here yet, surely he's set out from Asia? If he hasn't set out, surely at least he's thinking about it? What *is* he thinking about besides hunkering down on somebody else's goods, grabbing the harvest, plundering the fields, reducing the whole estate to a ruin? *He's* not stupid enough to prefer to come to Caesar and lose his case rather than stay in Asia and in possession.

If this rule becomes established, that the wills of decedents are to be sent from overseas provinces to Rome, the danger to these wills will be more disgraceful and more harsh than if it were the rule for the bodies of those who make wills overseas to be sent here. Bodies, at least, can now be in no danger any more. Burial is readily available to corpses in the very hazards of travel themselves. Whether the seas gulp them down, if they're shipwrecked, or rivers drag the bodies headlong, or the sands bury them, or the wild beasts tear them to bits, or the birds pick them apart, the human body is buried well enough wherever it's reduced to nothing.[8] But when a will goes down in a shipwreck, then once and for all that estate and household and family are shipwrecked and buried. Once upon a time wills were brought out of the most secure temples of the gods or registries or bank vaults or public record offices or back rooms of shrines; but now wills will have to set sail across a stormy sea, in with the load of cargo and the duffel bags of the rowers. All that's missing is this: if they need to lighten the load by throwing things overboard, for the wills to be thrown overboard along with the beans.[9] Maybe we should set up a customs tax on wills! . . . [a page is illegible here][10]

Let's say something about the funeral. The family should know how to mourn. A slave who's been manumitted laments differently, a client left something with compliments laments differently, a friend honored by a legacy laments differently.[11] Why make funeral ceremonies full of doubt and suspense? For all living things, their legacies are given out right after death: the sheepskin is stripped off the sheep right away, ivory off the elephant, claws off lions, feathers and down off birds; meanwhile human legacies after death just lie there, they get put off, they're left open to thieves and ripped to shreds.

I think I've written down the whole thing![12] Then what should I have done, when I was impressed with the whole thing, when I loved the whole lucky person? Good-bye, most eloquent, most erudite, dearest to me, sweetest, my most favorite teacher, most longed-for friend.

The son born to Herodes[13] today has died. Herodes is not taking this calmly.[14] I want you to write him something proper to the situation in a few words or so. Always be well.

Notes

1. shameless: Lat. *impudens,* a word that can have sexual overtones, e.g., "sluttish," "brazen." See n. 12, letter 20.

2. my father—my Lord: The emperor Antoninus Pius.

3. I even . . . performing: This is in Greek mixed with Latin in the original; the reference is to a theatrical performance. Oratorical training included much

that resembled theatrical training, and indeed orators often took lessons from famous actors, although this made them uneasy owing to the low social status of actors (see Richlin 1997). Fronto responds in letter 33 with an explicit comparison of Marcus to the actors Roscius and Aesopus. Note also Marcus and Fronto's recurring quotations from early Roman playwrights (see, e.g., letter 17 [Plautus and Naevius], letter 22 [Ennius, Plautus, Naevius, and Novius], letter 25 [Laberius]). The speech that Marcus goes on to transcribe deals with inheritance law, a topic normally exciting only to estate lawyers; but Marcus's selection is readily performable—dramatic, funny, and set up in short, speakable lines full of vivid and silly pictures. It is quite different from Fronto's letter-writing and essay styles, and different as well from all but the comic sections of Cicero's speeches (e.g., the scene in the baths in the *Pro Caelio*). Features common to Fronto's other styles that do show up in the speech include parataxis (a feature evidently copied from the elder Cato [see n. 6, letter 27]) and strings of nouns; there are several extended metaphors, recalling Fronto's beloved similes (see, e.g., letter 21). Note that Marcus has copied all this himself by hand (see letter 33; also letters 9, 18, 22, 40, and 41), and that, as Fronto makes clear in letter 33, Marcus is copying it from a set of extracts that Fronto had sent him in the first place.

4. "*Bravissimo!*": Lit. "In a manner worthy of the poet!" This is in Greek in the original.

5. from here: What follows is the only extant long fragment of a speech by Fronto.

6. writing fiction: Lat. *comminiscor;* see n. 8, letter 42, and note the connotation here of "telling a lie."

7. Asia: Asia Minor, the Near East.

8. reduced to nothing: This whole section is outrageous in ancient terms and would have been received with scandalized laughter. Proper burial in a family plot was important to the Romans, who were ancestor worshipers; burial at sea was thus especially abhorrent to them (although they worried about drowning while on a voyage, not about having their corpses carted off in a ship). All the eventualities that Fronto lists are commonplace terrors in epic poetry (e.g., *Iliad* 1.4–5, Achilles made many heroes "spoils for the dogs and birds"). The wording may also owe something to Lucretius and Epicurean ideas about the naturalness of the decomposition of the body. For a similar parody, see Petronius *Satyricon* 114–15.

9. with the beans: Lat. *cum leguminibus,* lit. "with the legumes." That cargo was jettisoned during storms and in the face of shipwreck was another commonplace, and hence figures in comic shipwrecks as at Juvenal *Satires* 12.33–47 (cf. Petronius *Satyricon* 103). Legumes are instanced here as lowly, also possibly recalling Pythagorean ideas about beans, vegetarianism, and the transmigration

of souls, which again show up in Roman comic writing (Juvenal *Satires* 3.228–29; 15.171–74, *non omne legumen*). Indeed, non-Pythagoreans as far back as Aristophanes found the Pythagoreans' vegetarianism hilarious; for a full list of sources, see Mayor's commentary on Juvenal at 15.171–74.

10. Yes, Marcus had copied out even more of this speech. Van den Hout (1988) prints what Hauler pieced together of the missing section; it seems to say that the testator was a *publicanus* (tax-contractor) and that the relatives contesting the will were his sisters, but its condition is too poor for translation.

11. differently: In other words, people who get something in a will mourn more energetically than those who don't, and the testator deserves credit.

12. the whole thing: That is, everything Fronto had extracted from the speech himself and sent to Marcus.

13. Herodes: See notes to letters 8–9, 12. Herodes was about to become one of Marcus's teachers.

14. calmly: This P.S. with its bald comment on the loss of a newborn child must strike a modern reader as odd. There is a large literature on the degree of grief felt by ancient people on the loss of young children in light of the high infant mortality rate (see Dixon 1997). On the expression of grief by Roman men, see Richlin 2001; on Herodes' peculiar grieving habits, see Holford-Strevens 1988, 101–3. But even if we accept the position that Greeks and Romans felt little grief on these occasions—which is undercut by many of the letters between Marcus and Fronto (see Haines 2.222–33 = *De nepote amisso* 2 = van den Hout, pp. 235–39; as well as letter 44)—or that Marcus was adhering to Stoic precepts on controlling emotion, this is an odd message coming from Marcus. Like the earlier letters about Herodes (8–10) and Julianus (11–12), this one involves a sort of homework assignment for Fronto; it elicited a fairly elaborate and not markedly cooperative letter from Fronto to Herodes (see letter 34).

Letter 33

To my Lord,

I received your letter, Caesar, and you may easily calculate exactly how much I was made happy by it if you count up the individual points. First, and this is the head of all my joy, that I know how well you are doing; then that I felt you to be so loving toward me that you set no boundary, no limit to your love, that would keep you from finding something more delightful and more loving to do for me every day. Finally, I thought I had long since been loved enough, but for you even as much as you love me it's still not enough yet; so that no sea is as deep as your love for me—so that I could really complain, why don't you already love me as much as ever you can, since by loving me more every day you prove that the love you gave me the day before wasn't the most possible.

Do you think that my consulship brought me as much joy as the proofs of your utmost love, so many of them in one place? The tidbits[1] of my speech that I'd excerpted you recited for your father yourself, and you took thought about the delivery, and by doing so you adapted your eyes and your voice and your gestures[2] and especially your mind for my use. I don't see any one of the classical[3] writers at all who was luckier than I am, even though Aesopus or Roscius[4] declaimed to the people what they had written. No, my speech had Marcus Caesar as its actor and declaimer, and I pleased my audience by means of your effort and voice, though to be your audience and to please you would be everybody's utmost wish. So I'm not surprised that a speech decorated[5] by the distinction of your lips gave pleasure. After all, many things that lack their own loveliness are lent a charm not their own from a source outside themselves. That's how it is even with those awful things the lower classes eat:[6] there's no potato or hot dog[7] so cheap or common that it wouldn't seem quite elegant if it were arranged on golden dishes. The same thing happens with flowers and garlands; they have one level of distinction [in Portunus Square][8] when they're sold by the flower sellers, another when they're offered by priests [in the temple].

And I am that much luckier than Hercules and Achilles were, because their arms and weapons were carried by Patricoles[9] and Philoctetes,[10] men much inferior to them in manhood; but my little mediocre speech, not to say ignoble, was lit up by Caesar, most learned and eloquent of all. Nor did any stage ever have such distinction— Marcus Caesar as the actor, Titus the emperor as the audience! What greater thing can happen to anyone, except the one that poets say happens in heaven, when the Muses sing with Father Jupiter as their audience? And what's more, what words could I use to express my joy that you sent me that old speech of mine written out by your own hand? It's certainly true, as our friend Laberius[11] says, that, to make someone fall in love, "baby talk is crazy talk, devotions are de-potions."[12] And nobody could ever have pounded such a flame into a lover by potion or love charm as you, by what you did, have made me dazed and thunderstruck by your burning love. For every letter on the page, that's how many consulships, that's how many laurels, triumphs, victory robes[13] I think I achieved.

What ever happened to Marcus Porcius like this?—or to Quintus Ennius, Gaius Gracchus, or the poet Titius, to Scipio or Numidicus? What ever happened to Marcus Tullius[14] like this? Yet their books are considered more valuable and hold the highest prestige when the copies are written by the hand of Lampadio or Staberius, Plautius or Decimus Aurelius, Autrico or Aelius, or edited by Tiro, or transcribed by Domitius Balbus or by Atticus or Nepos.[15] My speech will live on because it was written by the hand of Marcus Caesar. Why, even someone who scorns the oration will lust after[16] the letters;[17] someone who scorns what was written will hold in awe the one who wrote it down. Likewise if Apelles[18] painted a monkey or a fox, the painting would add value to the worthless animal; or what Marcus Cato <said> about the . . . [text breaks off here][19]

Notes

1. tidbits: Lat. *particulas*—the same word Fronto uses in letter 26 to describe the emotional nourishment provided by Marcus.

2. gestures: *Actio,* "body movement," was considered to be one of the chief branches of oratory. In this area in particular, rhetorical theorists compare oratory with drama (see Richlin 1997; also letter 32).

3. classical: Lat. *veterum,* "old"; cf. letters 20, 23.

4. Aesopus, Roscius: Clodius Aesopus and Quintus Roscius Gallus were the two most famous actors of the early first century BCE; Cicero himself studied with Roscius (see n. 3, letter 32). Roscius was famous for his rendition of the pimp Ballio in Plautus's *Pseudolus.* Marcus is said to have had lessons from the comic actor Geminus (*HA Life of Marcus* 2.2).

5. decorated: Lat. *exornata.* This verb means "ennoble, distinguish, glorify," but comes from *orno,* "decorate, adorn, costume (as for a play)." Plautus's comedies are full of plays on the word. So, here, *to decorate* is "to give a medal to" but also "to dress up, deck out."

6. those . . . eat: Lat. *in plebeis istis edulibus,* "in those [contemptuous] edibles of the plebs." *Edulia* is an unusual word, found in comedy and vernacular settings.

7. potato or hot dog: Lat. *holus aut pulpamentum. Holus* means "vegetable," but often (as here) a lowly or despised one, a generic that has no English equivalent, so *potato* is used here as an arbitrary example; *cabbage* would also do. *Pulpamentum,* "bits of meat eaten as a snack," is the name of a particular dish and shows up in Plautus and in later writers as a lowly food item. Again, *hot dog* is an arbitrary example; *beef jerky, hamburger, pork rinds,* or, in England, *pie* would also do. Cf. Ital. *polpetone,* "meat loaf."

8. in Portunus Square: Lat. *in Portunio.* This, with the phrase *in the temple* at the end of the sentence, may be a gloss (a note inserted by a later commentator). The flower market was near the temple of Portunus, the harbor god.

9. Patricoles: Patroclus was the best friend and comrade in arms of Achilles, the greatest hero of the Trojan War; in the *Iliad,* Achilles kills Hector in revenge for Hector's killing of Patroclus. Later Greek writers, most famously Plato, talk about the story that Achilles and Patroclus were lovers; Phaedrus, who is a character in Plato's *Symposium* as well as in the *Phaedrus,* has Achilles as the *erômenos* (*Symposium* 180a; see also Dover 1978, 196–99). The odd spelling of the name employed here is found in Ennius and Cicero and might, to a Roman reader, have the sound of a Latin compound noun formation—*Patri-cola,* "Father-worshiper"—which would suit the context.

10. Philoctetes: Philoctetes was the friend of Hercules and inherited his mighty bow on Hercules' death. He does not figure among several companions who are said to have been Hercules' *erômenoi* (see Dover 1978, 199). He was, however, famous for being lamed by a snakebite (see n. 24, letter 21), and is closely identified with the bow itself.

11. Laberius: For the comic playwright Laberius (first century BCE), see letter 25. This seems to be another loose quotation, here a verse with words missing.

12. baby talk ... de-potions: Lat. *delenimenta esse deleramenta, beneficia autem veneficia,* lit. "sweet talk is mad raving, kind deeds moreover (are) love potions." The effect in Latin is Cole Porter–ish. For the word *delenimenta* used by Fronto, see n. 9, letter 20; for *deleramenta* used by Marcus, see n. 19, letter 25. *Veneficia* translates literally as "poison-making" and represents a whole Roman concept of witchcraft as tied with poisoning, illicit love, and (mostly female) supernatural activities. On Marcus's "Thessalian love charms," see n. 19, letter 2.

13. victory robes: Lat. *togas pictas,* "embroidered togas." The general celebrating a triumph rode in a special chariot wearing the *toga picta* and a laurel crown. This purple toga was embroidered with gold stars. After the empire began, triumphs came to be considered the prerogative of the emperor (see Ando 2000, 285), so Fronto's metaphor here is a poignant one; consuls would now enjoy wearing these accessories in processions at the Circensian games (cf. Juvenal's bitter take on this, *Satires* 10.33–53, and Mayor's notes ad loc.). On Fronto's expressed preference for Marcus over his consulship, see letter 26.

14. Tullius: This ends a list of famous writers, most familiar already in this letter collection. Marcus Porcius is Cato (see n. 6, letter 7). Quintus Ennius is the great early Roman playwright and epic poet (see n. 3, letter 12). Gaius Gracchus is the politician and orator of the mid-republic (see n. 10, letter 12). The poet Titius is a tragic playwright whose works are now lost. Scipio is the great soldier and literary patron (see n. 14, letter 22). Numidicus must be Quintus Caecilius Metellus Numidicus, a controversial soldier and politician of the early first century BCE (not mentioned as a great orator by Cicero, but cited often by Fronto's acquaintance, Aulus Gellius). Marcus Tullius is Cicero; Fronto ends with the greatest orator.

15. Nepos: This ends a list of literary men, not all of them writers; they are much less famous than the writers who precede them in the letter, and some of them were not freeborn. Gaius Octavius Lampadio (second century BCE), probably a freed slave, is elsewhere associated with Ennius only by Fronto's acquaintance Aulus Gellius. Staberius Eros, a freed slave and grammarian (first century BCE), then seems to be matched here with Cato. Plautius may be the scholar Lucius Plotius Gallus (first century BCE); he seems to be matched with Gracchus, and Decimus Aurelius Opilius (early first century BCE) with Titius. Autrico is otherwise unknown, and presumably goes with Scipio; Lucius Aelius Stilo was a famous historian of language, friend of Numidicus (also his speechwriter), and teacher of Cicero. Marcus Tullius Tiro was the freed slave and secretary of Cicero who (possibly) collected Cicero's letters for publication. This Domitius Balbus is otherwise unknown. Titus Pomponius Atticus was Cicero's friend and corre-

spondent, also known as a writer of historical biography. Cornelius Nepos was Atticus's friend and wrote his biography as well as others'. James Zetzel (1973) has argued that what Fronto thinks these people did is not editorial work but just copying, and that, in any case, any such books would have been forgeries, unbeknownst to Fronto and Gellius.

Fronto adopts a highly risky strategy in this letter; it looks back to what he does in letter 2 with the *erôtikos logos,* and stands in sharp contrast with the letters in which he humbles himself (see n. 2, letter 24). He sets up a series of metaphors and analogies in which Marcus is likened to the low, secondary, and/or feminine: actors; sidekicks (and perhaps *erômenoi*); Muses; witches; someone trying to bewitch a "lover" (*amator*); conquered territory; editors and critics, some of them slaves or freedmen; a Greek painter. Perhaps this has something to do with the postscript on Herodes at the end of letter 32; letter 34, to Herodes, will show Fronto also trying to put his addressee in his place—and this in a condolence letter.

16. lust after: Lat. *concupiscet,* "desire ardently," "covet."

17. the letters: Probably "the individual letters in which each word is written" rather than "the letter you wrote." Note again the fetishizing of handwriting (see the volume introduction; and cf. letters 9, 12, 18, 22, 32, 40, and 41).

18. Apelles: The famous Greek painter (see n. 6, letter 23).

19. The whole last sentence is based on a barely legible section.

Letter 34

To Herodes from Fronto,[1]

[beginning of letter is lost] . . . and perhaps more . . . than us; to be calm in lesser misfortunes is not troublesome. After all, <to weep and wail> over <everything> every time and <carry on beyond what is fitting> is unseemly for a man <with experience> of education.[2] I would <rather> overstep the bounds of joy <than those of mourning>.[3] After all, a miscalculation on the side of pleasure is preferable to one on the side of grief. Moreover, the time of life[4] for raising children has not passed you by, either. Every loss that comes with the smiting of hope is hard to bear; but it's easier when hope is left of making good your loss. And the man who does not wait for it acts badly born,[5] and much harder on himself than Chance. After all, Chance bereaves a man of what he has, but this man has bereft himself even of hope.

Where may you most easily chance on comfort? I'll teach you, having learned it myself through experience and not by philosophy. It has always been my lot to suffer some hurt at the same time as I gave my heart.[6] At one time I was in love with the philosopher Athenodotus,[7] at another with Dionysius[8] the rhetor. In any case, I bore it in mind that the one I chanced to love was still mine, and so I was less easily a prey to grief and misfortunes. But if you, as I do, passionately love a certain wellborn young man, outstanding for his virtue and education and fortune and modesty,[9] you won't go wrong if you anchor yourself in him and place all your hope of good things in him, seeing that, as long as he is preserved to us—for I proclaim that I am your rival in love,[10] and make no secret of it—all our other problems can easily be healed and come a distant second to this.

Notes

1. To Herodes from Fronto: This letter is written in Greek; the original salutation is lost. For Herodes Atticus and Fronto's previous attitude toward him, see

letters 8–10 and 12. This is the letter of condolence on the death of Herodes' baby son requested by Marcus in letter 32.

2. <with experience> of education: Gk. *paideias <pepeir>amenôi*. The theme of teaching permeates this letter in a scarcely veiled statement by Fronto of his better claim to be Marcus's teacher. Here he means that Herodes has been educated and should therefore know better, but also that one who is about to take on a job as a teacher should know better.

3. I would . . . <than those of mourning>: The letter is full of philosophical commonplaces that would be at best tactless when offered to a man grieving for a child.

4. time of life: Herodes would have been about forty-two; he was about five years younger than Fronto.

5. badly born: Gk. *agennês*, "ignoble," "mean-spirited" (Haines). But the near homonym *agenês* means "unborn" or "childless," a subtly hurtful word choice. Van den Hout (1999, 43) labels this "one of Fronto's puns."

6. I gave my heart: Gk. *erônti*. The words for "love" in this part of the letter all come from *erôs*, "sexual love, desire." This is strong language and must here be a metaphor, though a daring one; by explicitly expressing the teacher/student relationship in terms of sexual love, Fronto was on dangerous ground. On gender politics in ancient education, see the volume introduction. No one knew better than Fronto that a metaphor, like a joke, can express its literal meaning within a framework that denies that this is what's being said (see letters 22 and 44).

7. Athenodotus: Fronto's teacher, a philosopher and rhetorician; he was a student of Musonius Rufus, who was one of the most eminent Roman Stoics and notable for his emphasis on marriage over pederasty (see the volume introduction). Marcus speaks of Athenodotus in the *Meditations* (1.13). See letter 44 at n. 2, where Fronto calls Athenodotus "teacher and father [*parenti*]" and says that Athenodotus taught him the theory of similes.

8. Dionysius: Fronto's teacher, otherwise known as the author of a literary commentary.

9. virtue . . . modesty: A typically Frontonian list, even in Greek.

10. rival in love: Gk. *anterastês*. Compare here the jockeying to gain the favor of an *erômenos* in letter 2. For the firmly pederastic context of the word *anterastês*, see Plato *Erastai* 132c; note the setting at a school.

\<Marcus Caesar to his teacher>,

. . . [indeterminate number of lines missing] and my personal trainer had me down by the gullet.[1] But what about the story, you ask? As my father was taking himself home from the vineyard, I mounted my horse as I usually do, and I set out on the road and rode out[2] a bit of a way. Well, there on the road a lot of sheep were all bunched up together, and they were standing there just the way they usually do in narrow places, and four dogs and two shepherds, but nothing else. Then one shepherd says to the other shepherd, when he sees a bunch of riders, "Hey, looky there at those damn[3] riders, because they're the kind that do the biggest rustling jobs." When I hear this, I dig my spurs into my horse and drive my horse into the sheep. The sheep get all excited and scatter, they run around every which way, straying and braying.[4] The shepherd hurls his fork at us—the fork hits the rider who was following me. We run away. That's how the guy who was afraid he'd lose his sheep lost his fork.[5] You think this is just a story? It's the real thing; but there was a lot more I could have written about this thing if the messenger weren't calling me now to take a bath. Good-bye, my sweetest teacher, most honorable and rarest person, my sweetness and dearness and pleasure.

Notes

1. personal . . . gullet: Lat. *meus me alipta faucibus urgebat.* The word *alipta,* here translated "personal trainer," is a Greek technical term, *aleiptês,* rarely adopted into Latin. It literally means "one who rubs with oil"; such a person would rub the body of a sick person, of an athlete in the wrestling school, or of a person in the baths, where the exercise was an optional precursor to the rub-down. He evidently might also serve as a general trainer. Transliterated into Latin this occupational title appears, before Marcus, only in a letter of Cicero, where it is parallel with *medici* (doctors), and in two satires of Juvenal, a contemporary of Marcus and Fronto. The satirical contexts are most illuminating. *Aliptes* (an alternate form) appears in a list of job titles that the abhorred Orient has poured into Rome, guises of the "hungry little Greek" (see n. 15, letter 9): schoolteacher,

rhetorician, geometry teacher, painter, augur, ropedancer, doctor, Oriental medicine man (Juvenal *Satires* 3.76–77). The list is contemptuous in content and
structure; elsewhere the *aleiptês* is clearly a slave. Note that Fronto's occupational
title, *rhetor,* is on this list. Juvenal also portrays a slave *aliptes* who "cannily presses
his fingers" into his female owner's *crista* (pussy; lit., cock's comb) after her bath
and weight-training workout, like a modern massage parlor worker (*Satires*
6.422). Marcus's description of himself with his *alipta,* then, has a whiff of the
racy/disreputable, and the *alipta* is someone far down on the social scale (compare the rest of the letter). This is also a story of the intimate care of the imperial
body. Judging by the position, this *alipta* seems to be wrestling with Marcus; on
the sexual connotations of wrestling, see n. 11, letter 2, and compare here esp.
Strato *Greek Anthology* 12.222. See Hubbard 2005 for the erotics of wrestling in
classical Greece.

   2. road and rode out: Marcus here has a jingle, *profectus,* "set out," and *provec-
tus,* "rode out."

   3. those damn: Lat. *istos,* "those [contemptuous]."

   4. straying and braying: Marcus makes a jingle here, *palantes balantesque,* lit.
"straying and baaing."

   5. fork: Lat. *furca.* Here a sort of sheep prod; the term *furca* was applied to a
variety of Y-shaped instruments, including one employed in a form of slave torture. These shepherds were probably slaves; for Marcus's attitude toward local
people, see n. 12, letter 39. Ramsay MacMullen chose this incident to begin his
book *Roman Social Relations;* his chapter on rural life makes an illuminating
background to Marcus's story here (1974, 1–27).

Letter 36

To my Lord,

I'm keeping myself in bed. If, when you're all going to Centum-cellae,[1] I could be fit for the journey, I'll see you at Lorium[2] on the ninth,[3] God willing.[4] Make my excuses to our Lord your father;[5] as I hope to see you all well, I love him and admire him a great deal more deeply because he gave such a good decision in the senate—one that'll both benefit the provinces and gently rebuke the defendants.

When you hold the grand opening of the game preserve, just re-member as hard as you possibly can that, if you're stabbing at wild beasts, you should give your horse free rein. You'll certainly produce Galba[6] at Centumcellae. Or will you be able to do the eighth at Lorium? Good-bye, Lord, keep your father happy, say hello to your mother, miss me. What Cato[7] has to say about how Galba got off[8] you know better than I do; I recall that he was exonerated because of his brother's sons. Check it out *exactement*[9] yourself. Cato as a result argues that nobody should produce children in court to arouse pity—not their own or anybody else's, not wives or relatives or any women at all. Say hello to your lady mother.

Notes

1. Centumcellae: See n. 1, letter 7.

2. Lorium: A town on the Via Aurelia, which was the road that led from Rome northwest along the coast of Etruria, passing through Centumcellae.

3. on the ninth: Lit. "on the seventh day before the Ides." The month in which this letter was written is not known, so, by the Roman system, the date could be the seventh or the ninth. Below, Fronto makes it a day earlier.

4. God willing: Lit. "if the gods are favorable."

5. father: Antoninus Pius, the emperor.

6. Galba: See n. 8 below.

7. Cato: See n. 6, letter 7.

8. how Galba got off: Cato spoke against Servius Sulpicius Galba at a public hearing in 149 BCE at which Galba was accused of misconduct as governor of

Lusitania (now Portugal). Van den Hout points out (1999, 141) that Fronto has not in fact remembered correctly and that it was his own two sons and a young relative whom Galba used in court. This kind of emotional grandstanding is commonly attested in Cicero's speeches.

9. *exactement:* Lit. "the exact thing." This is in Greek in the original.

Letter 37

Marcus Caesar to Marcus Fronto his teacher, hello,

After I got in the wagon, after I said good-bye to you, we had, not too bad a journey, but we were a tiny bit spattered by a shower. But before we came to the villa, we took a detour to Anagnia,[1] about a mile off the road. Then we took a tour of that ancient town, a tiny little place of course, but it has lots of ancient things in it—temples and holy rituals over the top. There wasn't a corner where you wouldn't find a shrine or a sanctuary or a temple. Also many books written on linen, which has to do with religious rules. Then there in the gateway, as we were leaving, words had been written twofold as follows: "Flamen,[2] put on the *samentum*." I asked one of the locals what that last word might be. He said that in the language of the Hernici[3] it meant the skin of the sacrificial victim, which the flamen puts on his *apex*[4] when he enters the city. We learned quite a lot of other things we wanted to know; but there's one thing we don't want—that you're away from us—that's the biggest thing we're worried about.

Now you—after you set out from there, did you go to the Aurelia[5] or to Campania?[6] Make sure you write and tell me, and whether you've begun the vintage, and whether you've brought a huge number of books to the villa, and this too, whether you long for me—which it's stupid for me to ask for, when you do it by yourself. Now you—if you long for me and if you love me, you must send me your letters often, because it knits up my ravell'd sleave of care.[7] For I'd ten times rather pick through[8] your letters than all the grapevines of Mt. Massicus or Mt. Gaurus;[9] for these awful ones from Signia[10] really have too-gross grapes and sour seeds—I'd rather drink it as wine than as grape juice.[11] Besides it's much pleasanter to gobble those grapes when they're dried than when they're juicy; indeed I'd much rather stamp them with my feet than nibble them with my teeth. But still, may they favor and forgive me, and bestow their kind mercy upon me in return for all this teasing. Be well for me, person most loving, most delicious, most eloquent, sweetest teacher. When you see the new wine seething in the cask, let it remind you that, for me, that's the way the longing for you bubbles and overflows and makes foam in my heart. Always be well.

Notes

1. Anagnia: A town in Latium, just off the Via Latina, and east of Signia (see n. 10 below). Marcus's antiquarian tourism here is notable and was fastened on by its ideal reader, Walter Pater, who makes a teasing allusion to this letter in chap. 27 of *Marius the Epicurean* (see the volume introduction).

2. Flamen: A Roman priest title, here in use in Anagnia as well. Flamens performed the rituals for particular gods; e.g., the flamen Dialis at Rome was the priest of Jupiter. Flamens were subject to many and peculiar religious restrictions as to behavior and dress.

3. Hernici: One of the peoples of Latium, the area around Rome. The Roman expansion in the Italian peninsula included the conquest or absorption of many local cultures; this then is a survival.

4. *apex:* Flamens wore a sort of skullcap, the *pilleus,* with a point (the *apex*) protruding from it. A man wearing this headgear appears on the Ara Pacis.

5. to the Aurelia: Lat. *in Aureliam.* Marcus seems to mean the area around the Via Aurelia (see n. 2, letter 36).

6. Campania: The area around the Bay of Naples, famous for its lush productivity and comfortable life.

7. knits up . . . care: Lat. *solacium atque fomentum sit,* "it's my consolation and cold compress." This is a rough quotation from Cicero, *Tusculan Disputations* 2.59, where it appears in a lofty description of how the wise man can refrain from feeling pain. In this context, it is somewhat flippant.

8. pick through: Marcus puns on two meanings of *legere,* "pick" and "read."

9. all the grapevines of Mt. Massicus or Mt. Gaurus: These are mountains in Campania—one of the places where Marcus thinks Fronto might be—famous for good wines. A translation rendered in contemporary terms might be "all the grapevines of Napa or Sonoma."

10. Signia: The wine of Signia was bitter and used medicinally. Marcus may have been writing from Signia, since it is not far from Anagnia.

11. I'd . . . grape juice: Lit. "I'd rather drink the wine than the must," i.e., rather the wine that's been around a while, fermenting, than the (ordinarily sweet) new wine or grape juice. It's hard to avoid the feeling that Marcus is not talking just about grapes here and in what follows, especially when he soon afterward calls Fronto both *suavissime,* "most delicious," and *dulcissime,* "sweetest."

Letter 38

Hi my teacher most serious,[1]

We're all well. Today I personally studied from three in the morning until eight a.m., having cleverly arranged for some food; from eight to nine I puttered around very happily outside, by my bedroom, in my slippers. Then I put my boots on and took my army jacket[2]—that's how we were notified to come—and I went off to say my hello to my Lord.

We set out for the hunt, we did deeds of derring-do, we heard (by declaration) that boars had been captured, for indeed there was no way we were going to see any. But we climbed a steep enough hill; then in the afternoon we marched ourselves back home. And me—back to my little books. So, boots hauled off, clothes dumped, I lingered in bed nearly two hours. I read Cato's speech[3] "On the Goods of Pulchra" and another one in which he indicted a tribune. "Hey!"[4] you're saying to your boy.[5] "Go as fast as you can, bring me back these speeches from the Library of Apollo."[6] You're wasting your time, because those same sorry books have followed me too. So you'll have to feel up[7] the librarian at the Tiberian Library[8] and money's going to have to change hands to take care of this—he can divvy it up with me when I get back to Rome. But me—speeches read, I wrote a tiny bit, poorly, something for me to donate to the water nymphs or the fire god:[9] "truly ill-fated did I write this day,"[10] definitely a hunter's scribble, or a grape picker's—they make my bedroom clang with their yodeling,[11] absolutely boring and tedious, just lawyeresque.[12] But what have I said? No, I haven't said the wrong thing, because my teacher, obviously, is an Orator.

I seem to have caught myself a cold—because I walked around in slippers in the morning, or because I wrote badly, I don't know. Certainly I'm a runny-nosed person as a general rule, but today I feel much more snot-laden.[13] So I'll pour the oil on my head[14] and commence to sleep; for I'm planning not to put a drop of it into my lamp today, equitation and sneezitation made me so tired. You'll be well for me, won't you, dearest and sweetest teacher, whom I dare say I long for more than Rome itself.

Notes

1. most serious: Lat. *gravissime*. A variant reading—*carissime,* "dearest"—is noted on the margin of the manuscript.

2. army jacket: Lat. *sagulo. A sagum* was a wool military cloak, a style borrowed from the northern barbarians; a *sagulum* was presumably a short one. Or this may just be more of Marcus's facetiousness: "my tiny army coat."

3. Cato's speech: No fragments of this speech or the other mentioned here are preserved, and the first is known only by this mention. For Cato, see n. 6, letter 7.

4. Hey: Lat. *Io.*

5. boy: The word "boy" in Latin often, as here, means "slave."

6. Library of Apollo: Situated on the Palatine Hill in Rome, and inaugurated by Augustus in 28 BCE, this library housed a huge collection of Latin literature.

7. you'll have to feel up: Lat. *subigitandus est. Subigito* and its related forms denote genital stimulation with the hands; the tone is coarse, the sense often tied in with prostitution, as at Plautus *Persa* 227. Alternative translations would be "massage," "fondle," "jerk off."

8. Tiberian Library: The library of the House of Tiberius, where Marcus lived. This library is less important than the Library of Apollo (see n. 6 above) and is mentioned here and only twice elsewhere.

9. water nymphs, fire god: Lat. *lymphis* and *Volcano;* i.e., the garbage. For Marcus's tendency to destroy his own work, see letter 22.

10. "truly . . . day": In Greek in the original, and metrical; as the text stands, this is an iambic line, slightly off (like most lines of verse Marcus quotes). The Greek is *alêthôs atuchôs sêmeron gegraptai moi;* Jeffrey Henderson (personal communication) kindly points out that if the first two words were transposed this would be a line of choliambic verse, and that the two words, so similar in appearance, might well have been written in the wrong order by a scribe. Or, I would add, by Marcus himself. If this is a quotation, the source is unknown, but based on the content it would probably be from a comedy. But compare letter 19 at n. 6, where Marcus lapses into verse in the prosiest of contexts. The letters are full of references to his own efforts in poetry; like the poet Pope, he just may not have been able to help himself.

11. yodeling: Lat. *iubilis,* "songs/yells of fieldworkers." The same word recurs in letter 39, where Marcus boasts that he has joined in.

12. lawyeresque: Lat. *causidicali* (another rare word, used only here and by Fronto's acquaintance Aulus Gellius). On *causidici,* see n. 5, letter 26.

13. runny-nosed . . . snot-laden: Lat. *pituitosus . . . mucculentior.* Compare

Catullus 23, an invective poem in which Catullus accuses his friend Furius of being so poor that he even lacks "phlegm and bad snot of the nose" (*mucusque et mala pituita nasi,* line 17).

14. pour . . . head: The medical writer Celsus (first century CE) advises a person with a cold to pour hot salt water over his head, then rub his head vigorously and coat it with hot oil and wrap it up (4.2.7).

Letter 39

Hi my sweetest teacher,

We're all well. I slept a bit late because of my tiny little chill,[1] which seems to have calmed down. So from five a.m. to nine a.m. I partly read from Cato's *Agriculture*[2] and partly wrote, less lamely— lordy![3]—than yesterday. Then after I said good morning to my father, I "coddled my chops" with honey water by sucking it into my gullet and then tossing it out again—far be it from me to say "I gargled"—it's in Novius,[4] I think, and other places. But after tending to my chops I went off to my father[5] and stood by him while he performed the sacrifice. Then it was time for the morning break. What do you think I had for my snack? A tiny little bit of bread, while I watched everybody else gobbling up beans and onions and sardines, big pregnant ones.[6] Then we went to work to harvest the grapes and we sweated and yodeled and, as the poet[7] says, "We left some high-hung ones, survivors of the vintage." Just after noon we came back home.

I studied a tiny bit, and pretty stupidly. Then I had quite a chat with my mom,[8] who was sitting on the bed.[9] I'm all like: "What do you think my Fronto is doing now?" And she's like: "So what do you think my Cratia's[10] doing?" Then I'm: "But what about little Cratia,[11] our teeny-weeny little sparrow?" While we're going on like this and arguing about which of us loves which of you more, the gong boomed, which means notice was given that my father had gone to have a bath. So we had a bath and ate dinner in the winepress shed—I don't mean we had a bath in the winepress shed, but we had a bath and then ate dinner; and we had a good time listening to the yokels insulting each other for fun.[12] After I'm back in my room, before I turn myself on my side to snore, I untangle my yarn load[13] and render up an accounting of my day to my sweetest teacher—if I could long for him more, I'd gladly waste away a tiny bit more. Will you keep well for me, Fronto, wherever you are, my

honeyest honey, my love, my pleasure? What is it with me and you?
I love someone and he's not here.

Notes

1. tiny little chill: Lat. *perfrictiunculam.* Marcus loves diminutive forms, in this letter more than ever. They are characteristic of colloquial speech in Latin and are common in Plautus's comedies and Cicero's letters, but in Marcus they reach the level of a stylistic tic, possibly sarcasm.

2. Cato's *Agriculture:* For Cato, see n. 6, letter 7. *On Agriculture* is the only one of Cato's works still extant as a whole; it is a farming handbook, studied today (and probably by Marcus) mostly for its archaizing style. Ironically, it is full of practical directions for the vintage.

3. less . . . lordy: Lat. *minus misere mercule,* "less poorly, by Hercules."

4. Novius: Marcus is using a phrase from comedy, *fauces fovi* ("I coddled my chops") and rejecting the word *gargarissavi* ("I gargled"), a Greek word Latinized as a medical term. For Novius, see n. 12, letter 22.

5. father: Antoninus Pius, the emperor.

6. sardines, big pregnant ones: Lat. *maenas bene praegnatas. Maenae* are small fish attested as poor folks' food (*Oxford Latin Dictionary,* s.v.). By referring to them as *bene praegnatas,* lit. "well pregnant," Marcus may mean that they are full of fish eggs.

7. the poet: Novius, whom Marcus has just mentioned, wrote a play called *Harvesters,* so maybe this line came from there.

8. mom: Lat. *matercula,* an affectionate diminutive of *mater,* "mother."

9. with . . . bed: Lat. *cum matercula mea supra torum sedente.* Readers have repeatedly interpreted this to mean that Marcus studied in his own room and then went to visit his mother in her room: McQuige 1824, 87, "sitting with my dear mother on a couch, I prattled of many things"; Farrar 1874, 273, "I had a long talk with my mother, who was lying on her couch" (complete with line drawing by the illustrator of *The Princess and the Goblin*); Brock 1911, 45, "Now he describes his daily life at home, his long talks by his mother's sofa." But Marcus often studies in bed (see letters 4, 7, 31, and 38), and it seems more natural to understand that Domitia Lucilla has come into his room. *Torus* = a bed or the pillows and cushions that go on a bed. Cf. Suetonius *Domitian* 11.1.

10. Cratia: Fronto's wife.

11. little Cratia: Fronto's daughter.

12. yokels . . . fun: Lat. *rusticos cavillantes.* A whole genre of Golden Age scenes in Latin lies behind this phrase, along with two millennia of its descendants, from toile to folk music. Like other elite Romans, the royal family evidently got a kick

out of rural tourism. Yokels similarly entertain an august tour group with an insult match at Horace *Satires* 1.5.51–70; these insults followed a traditional format. For Marcus's run-in with some other agricultural workers, see letter 35.

13. my yarn load: Lat. *meum pensum,* an idiom for a day's allotted work, based on women's traditional household job of spinning wool. This metaphor, with the one that follows it, seems to describe not only Marcus thinking over his day, but also Marcus writing this letter, and perhaps has sexual overtones as well (cf. Aristophanes *Lysistrata* 729–34).

Letter 40

Hi teacher sweetest to me,

Finally the courier's setting out, and I can finally send off to you my minutes of the last three days. But I'm not saying anything— that's how much breath I spent on dictating almost thirty letters.[1] Actually your dictum about letters from last time I haven't yet repeated to my father.[2] But when, God willing, we come to the city,[3] remind me to tell you something about this issue: but you and I are both so spacey,[4] you won't remind me and I won't tell you the story— so we really do need to make a special plan. Good-bye my—what should I say? Whatever I say, it isn't enough—good-bye, my desire, <my light>, my pleasure.[5]

Notes

1. dictating . . . letters: On these letters as largely autograph and the fetishizing of handwriting, see the volume introduction.

2. father: The emperor, Antoninus Pius.

3. the city: Rome.

4. you and I . . . spacey: Lit. "such is your and my *meteoria*"; Gk. *meteôria* = "up-in-the-clouds-ness." This word appears only in the life of Claudius by Fronto's contemporary Suetonius (39.1) and here—not in any Greek authors— but Suetonius makes a point of it as a Greek word and the equivalent of what he has just described as Claudius's *oblivio*.

5. desire . . . pleasure: Cicero addresses his wife Terentia from exile with similar phrases: *mea lux, meum desiderium* (*Letters to His Friends* 14.2.2); so also the slave woman Chrysis to Encolpius (Petronius *Satyricon* 139.4) in a decidedly erotic context. But the words "my light" here are Mai's guess at filling in an illegible bit.

Letter 41

FRONTO TO MARCUS, ? 143-45 CE

To my Lord,

I've received your letter, so elegantly written, in which you say that because of the hiatus a longing for my letters has risen in you. Then it's true, what Socrates said—that pleasures are closely tied to pains—when he was in prison and balancing the pain of the tight shackle against the pleasure when it was taken off.[1] And so it's certainly the same for us: as much annoyance as absence brings us, we get just as much benefit from the longing it arouses. After all, longing comes from love. So our love has been made greater by longing, and this is by far the best thing in friendship. Then what you want to know about my health, I'd written to you before that I was indeed so terribly troubled by the pain of my shoulder that I couldn't do the job of writing that very letter in which I was telling you about it; but I was using <the hand of another>, contrary to our usual practice . . .[2]

Notes

1. Socrates . . . taken off: The idea ascribed to Socrates comes from the beginning of Plato's *Phaedo* (60b), loosely translated into Latin. What Socrates actually says is thought-provoking for Marcus and Fronto's relationship: that pleasure is an odd thing, strangely related to pain, and that a man who pursues one will have to encounter the other. The association between love and longing forms one of the major arguments in Plato's *Symposium*. Note Fronto's image of himself here again as Socrates (see letter 2) and as wearing shackles, like a slave (cf. letter 24).

2. The manuscript breaks off here. It again testifies to Fronto's practice of writing to Marcus himself rather than dictating a letter (see the volume introduction; and cf. letters 9, 12, 18, 22, 32, 33, and 40).

Letter 42

MARCUS TO FRONTO, BETWEEN APRIL 26, 146,
AND APRIL 26, 147 CE

To my teacher,[1]

Gaius Aufidius[2] is putting on airs, he's praising his talent for ar-
bitration sky-high, he denies that a more righteous man than he—
let's not go overboard here—ever came out of Umbria[3] to Rome.
Need you ask? He'd rather be praised as a judge than as an orator.
When I laugh at him, he looks down his nose at me; he says it's easy
for a yawning man to be assessor for a judge, but to be a real judge
is a splendid line of work. So much for me. But still the deal turned
out swell. Fine—I'm happy.

Your arrival makes me feel lucky and worried at the same time.
Why it should make me feel lucky, no one needs to ask; why it worries me I'll confess to you, honest to God. Because—what you gave
me to write[4]—I haven't put even the tiniest bit of work into it—
however little I had to do. The works of Ariston[5] are treating me well
this season, and then again they have me in bad shape: when they
teach me better, obviously then they're treating me well; but when
they truly show me how far my character is left behind by these better ideas, your student all too often blushes and disapproves of himself, seeing that now, at twenty-five years of age, I still haven't ab-
sorbed any right thinking and purer ideas into my soul. And so I
punish myself, I get mad, I'm sad, I'm envious,[6] I go without food.
While I've been tied up in these worries, every day now I've been
putting off the duty[7] of writing to the next day. But I'll make something up[8] soon; and as some Attic orator[9] advised the assembly
of the Athenians, "Sometimes you have to let the laws sleep." I'll
give the works of Ariston a little rest, now that I've paid my respects
to them, and I'll totally turn myself over to that actors' poet[10] of yours,
though first I'll read the Tullian mini-speeches.[11] But I'll write on
one side or the other, because—when it comes to holding different
views on the same thing—Ariston is absolutely never going to sleep

so soundly that he'd allow *that*.[12] Good-bye, my best and most honored teacher. My Lady[13] says hello.

Notes

1. To my teacher: At this point Marcus has dropped the long, affectionate salutations that characterize his earlier letters.

2. Gaius Aufidius: Victorinus, Marcus's friend and Fronto's future son-in-law (see n. 1, letter 20).

3. Umbria: A region northeast of Rome, something of a backwater; a tombstone of one of the descendants of Fronto and Victorinus was found at Pisaurum, a small city on the Umbrian coast. Plautus was said to have come from Umbria.

4. what you gave me to write: Fronto is still sending Marcus homework assignments. As the letter goes on to show, the one in question is a standard Roman rhetorical assignment, to take a case and argue both sides of it, as in the *Controversiae* of the elder Seneca. Compare letter 1, where Marcus is dealing with a similarly standard sort of assignment; now he's balking.

5. Ariston: A Stoic philosopher (third century BCE), pupil of Zeno, the founder of Stoicism. He focused on ethics, for which he placed great responsibility on the individual. There is a brief ancient biography by Diogenes Laertius (*Lives of the Philosophers* 7.160–64), where *Erôtikai diatribai* (*Discourses on Love*) are listed among his works. On Stoicism, see the volume introduction. Champlin (1974, 144) argues that Marcus here refers not to the philosopher but to a legal expert of the same name, which would limit this letter's focus to law; but the emotive language Marcus uses of his reactions to Ariston makes that seem doubtful.

6. I'm envious: Gk. *zêlotupô.*

7. duty: Lat. *obsequium.* This was the word used of the duty of obedience owed by a freed slave to his master; contrast Marcus's attitude toward his homework in the early letters.

8. make something up: Lat. *comminiscar,* the meanings of which shade from invention into falsehood (see n. 6, letter 32).

9. some Attic orator: The line quoted is, oddly, in Latin. This may be the saying attributed to the Spartan king Agesilaus by Fronto's contemporary Plutarch (*Agesilaus* 30.4); if so, this is another quotation error by Marcus. It would be interesting to know whether Marcus read Plutarch's life of Agesilaus, who is presented as a model king—raised with ordinary Spartan boys in their rigorous training, lovable, charming—even though lame. The biography leads with an explanation of why his *erastês* loved him.

10. that actors' poet: Haines "your stage poet"; Marcus and Fronto often discuss the work of Roman dramatists, who all wrote in verse (see n. 3, letter 32). Com-

pare letter 23 at n. 13, where Marcus is reading "Novian mini-farces and the mini-speeches of Scipio." But this is an odd phrase, and the text may just be corrupt.

11. Tullian mini-speeches: On "Tullian" (i.e., Ciceronian), see n. 17, letter 20. On "mini-speeches," see n. 13, letter 22.

12. But . . . *that:* This is the fatal line—this marks the end of Marcus and rhetoric. If doing philosophy meant no writing on both sides of an argument, then rhetoric became impossible. Marcus had numerous other teachers (*Meditations* 1); his main philosophy teacher was another ex-consul, Quintus Junius Rusticus, who is conspicuous by his absence from the Marcus-Fronto letters and from Fronto's correspondence as a whole (see Champlin 1980, 53, 106–7, 119–20). Rusticus appears only, and as a bit player, in a late letter, full of nostalgia for Marcus as orator, in which the orator is again, figuratively, ambiguously, kissed by his loving critic (Haines 2.32–47, at pp. 42–43 = *Ant. imp.* 1.2 = van den Hout, pp. 86–91 at p. 89, lines 14–15). For doubts that letter 42 is so significant, see Champlin 1974, 144; 1980, 121–22; and n. 5 above.

13. Lady: Probably here now Marcus's wife, Faustina, whom he married in 145.

Letter 43

FRONTO TO MARCUS, ? BETWEEN APRIL 26, 146,
AND APRIL 26, 147 CE

To my Lord,

The day after tomorrow, Lord, I'll see you; for I'm still ailing in my elbow and neck. Put up with me, I beg you, when I ask too many hard things of you: I have so gotten it into my head that you can accomplish as much as you try to do. I don't pray for you not to hate me,[1] if you haven't completed as much as I request, if you've put your mind and effort into it, as you do.[2] Good-bye, Lord; you count more to me than my soul. Say hello to your lady mother.

Notes

1. I don't pray . . . me: These lines perhaps faintly echo Catullus 76.23–26, where the poet prays to be released from a love he can no longer bear.

2. if you haven't . . . do: This letter appears to be written in response to letter 42, although there is no firm evidence one way or the other.

Letter 44

FRONTO TO MARCUS, 148 CE

Fronto to Caesar,

Good God, how thrown I was when I read the beginning of your letter! The way it was written made me worry it meant that you were the one whose health was in some danger. Then after you made it clear that the danger I'd understood as yours from the beginning of your letter was to your daughter Faustina, how my terror was transformed! Not just transformed, but even—I don't know how—somewhat lightened. All right, you may be saying: "My daughter's danger seemed less important to you than mine? That's how it seemed to you, when you're the one who's always announcing that Faustina, to you, is a cloudless sky, a holiday, hope close at hand, a wish come true, a total joy, an excellent and flawless source of pride?" But I do know what came to me as I was reading your letters; what was the reason it came out that way I truly don't know; I don't know, I'm saying, why I was thrown more by your danger than by your daughter's; unless maybe, even if they're equal, still things seem heavier when they first strike our ears. What might then be the reason for this, you'd know sooner than I would, since you know a good bit more about the nature and feelings of human beings and have been a better student.[1] I was taught in a middling sort of way by my teacher and father Athenodotus[2] about making models and certain images of things, which he called *eikones*,[3] that would be easily comprehensible and geared to the appropriate level; and so I seem to have found this image of this thing—I mean, of why my transferred fear might seem lighter to me: it's like what usually happens with people carrying a heavy burden on one shoulder. When they've transferred the same burden from the right shoulder to the left one, though nothing is subtracted from the weight, still this transfer of the burden also seems like a lightening.

Now since, in the last part of your letter, where you announced that Faustina was doing a little better now, you've absolutely put aside all my fear and worry, it seems that it might not be the wrong

LETTER 44 · 143

time to have a little chat[4] with you about my love for you, quite informally and man to man.[5] After all, it's pretty much a given that people who've been unburdened of great fear and terror are allowed to have a little fun[6] and play the fool.[7] I feel how dearly I love you no less[8] in time of heavy and serious trials than in many things that are even trivial. What things, or what kind of things, these trifles might be, I'll show you.

If ever I see you in my dreams, when I am "bound down," as the poet says, "in slumber gentle and calm," there's never a time when I'm not putting my arms around you and kissing you thoroughly:[9] then, according to the plot of whatever dream it is, I either weep profusely[10] or dance with some sort of happiness and pleasure. This is one plotline of my love, taken from the *Annals,*[11] a poetic one, and pretty dreamy. Here's another one, and this one's quarrely and fighty.[12] On several occasions I've laced into you behind your back, in rather serious terms, when I'm with my very few closest friends: sometimes this happened when you were going around with a more depressed attitude than was right for a gathering of folks, or when you were reading books at the theater or at a banquet—at that point I was not yet staying away from theaters and banquets—so then I used to call you "a hard person with no sense of what's appropriate," even "a hateful person," on several occasions when I was pushed to it by anger.[13] But if anybody else manhandled you in my hearing with the same terms of abuse, I couldn't hear it and stay calm. It was that much easier for me to speak myself than to allow others to say anything bad about you, just as I could more easily hit my daughter Cratia[14] myself than see her hit by another.

I'll add a third example from my list of trifles. You know how in all the banks and stands and storefronts and shops and arcades and entryways and windows, everywhere and every moment, images of you all are displayed to the public[15]—they're badly painted, sure, and most of them are shaped or carved under the inspiration of a thick, or I should say a mud-caked Muse;[16] but when your image, no matter how unlike you, catches my eye on my way, this never happens without jolting from my mouth the gape and dream of a kiss.[17]

Now to tally up my trifles and return to what's important, this letter of yours was most of all a proof to me of how dearly I love you, since I was more shaken up over your danger than your daughter's— though in general while of course I'd want you to survive me, truly I'd also want your daughter to survive you, as is right. But, hey, you see to it that you don't turn me in or testify against me to your daughter—as if I could really hold you more dear than her. For there's a danger that your daughter, riled up by this, since she's a se-rious and old-fashioned woman, might be quite angry over it and take away her hands and feet from me for kissing when I ask for them, or offer them only a bit grudgingly; while I, good God! will more gladly give a thorough kissing to her tiny little hands and those tiny little fat feet than to your royal neck[18] and your mouth, so sober and clever.

Notes

1. you know . . . better student: This seems to be a dig at Marcus's interest in philosophy; Marcus's preference for philosophy over rhetoric was firming up during this period (see letter 42). A certain degree of hostility shows through in many parts of the letter, combined with an unusual amount of waffling language. Marcus's first child, Faustina, was born in November 147, putting this letter in late 147 or 148.

2. Athenodotus: See n. 7, letter 34.

3. models . . . *eikones:* Fronto here sets up a metaphor about metaphors, us-ing language shared by natural philosophy and rhetoric. Athenodotus was a philosopher, not a rhetorician, and the *eikones* that he taught Fronto about could have come from optical or cognitive theory as well as from rhetoric (where *eikones* are similes, Fronto's specialty). This is fancy footwork, calculated to impress. The whole argument about the transferred fear is a pastiche of philosophical style and obviously disingenuous (note the crack about Marcus's knowledge of human na-ture), as the rest of the letter makes clear: Fronto loves Marcus much more than he loves the little girl. Note his use of *imagines,* "images," here and in the section where he talks about literal images of Marcus and their effect on him; this word has a rich range of meanings, including "duplicate," "reflection," "imitation," "ghost," "ancestor mask," and, in Epicurean philosophy, "an image emitted by an object and apprehended by the eyes" (*Oxford Latin Dictionary,* s.v.). Worth quot-ing on this Epicurean concept is Cicero *Lucullus* (*Prior Academics*) 125: "*imagines* break into our minds from outside through our bodies." Dreams are dealt with

as *imagines* in bk. 4 of Lucretius's *On the Nature of Things,* a most thought-provoking text to read with this one. The image of the shifted burden also shows up in Roman law, in the sections that deal with injury through negligence (*Digest* 9.2.7.1–2); Fronto, an eminent litigator, may also have this model in mind.

4. have a . . . chat: Lat. *fabulandi,* which also means "tell a story," "act out a play": Fronto is using theatrical language.

5. quite . . . man to man: Lat. *liberalius.* This is an odd word choice. *Liberalis* means "befitting a freeborn person" and is commonly used as a class marker, as in "like gentlemen." Compare the quotation below, "bound down in slumber," and the image of shackles as employed elsewhere (letters 14, 24, and 41). Perhaps translate as *unconstrainedly.*

6. have . . . fun: Lat. *ludere;* more theatrical language.

7. play the fool: Lat. *ineptire;* this word ends the first line of Catullus 8, "Poor Catullus, stop playing the fool," a poem in which the poet tries to talk himself out of loving his faithless girlfriend and ends by imagining her kisses.

8. no less: This seems like a slip for *no more;* or, as van den Hout says (1999, 182), it just means "as much." But, as Fronto says, read on.

9. putting . . . thoroughly: Lat. *amplectar et exosculer* (for this word, see end of this letter, and letter 45).

10. profusely: Lat. *ubertim,* which appears in a poem by Catullus (66.17) to describe the tears of a bride.

11. *Annals:* An epic poem by Ennius, a favorite writer of Fronto's (see n. 3, letter 12). This line might come from the lost lead-in to the dream of Ilia in *Annales* 1, in which case Fronto would be putting himself in the place of a female character (which he explicitly does in letter 45)—and one who has an important erotic dream of rape and abandonment at that. But most of Ennius's *Annales* is lost, so who knows. For the wording, cf. Ovid *Fasti* 3.11–28.

12. dreamy, quarrely, fighty: Lat. *somniculosus, rixatorium, iurgiosum.* These words are made up out of normal Latin nouns meaning "dream," "quarrel," and "fight." Word formations like this are a favorite device in Plautus, one of Fronto's favorite writers. *Iurgiosum* at least is not unique to Fronto, although it is characteristic of his period: it shows up in Gellius, Apuleius, in some grammarians, in Firmicus Maternus, and in the letters of Fronto's later fan Sidonius Apollinaris. But the sequence suggests that Fronto is deliberately making a cute jingle in order to tone down what he's about to say.

13. anger: This section sounds very much as if Fronto is worried that word of what he said had gotten back to Marcus. It seems out of place in a list of "trifles," and would certainly be tactless to bring up if Fronto didn't think Marcus knew about it—unless he wanted to upbraid Marcus in the guise of a joke.

14. my daughter Cratia: Now about six years old.

15. images . . . displayed to the public: These are images of the imperial family. On this aspect of Roman popular culture, see Ando 2000, 232–39.

16. Muse: Lit. *Minerva.* She was the patron goddess of artisans; van den Hout (1999, 184) translates her name as *art.*

17. gape and dream of a kiss: Lat. *rictum osculi et somn<i>um.* Van den Hout prints *iactum osculi et savium,* "a blown kiss and a soul kiss," but calls this "a desperate effort" (1999, 185). The text as is seems harshly worded but striking, and it well recalls the first of Fronto's "trifles"; it also echoes a pederastic kiss poem in an anecdote recorded by Fronto's acquaintance Aulus Gellius (19.11.4):

Dum semihiulco savio	*While with half-wide-open kiss*
meum puellum savior	*I kiss my laddie,*
dulcemque florem spiritus	*and I take the sweet flower*
duco ex aperto tramite,	*of his breath from the open stream-way,*
anima aegra amore et saucia	*my soul, lovesick and wounded,*
cucurrit ad labeas mihi,	*has run to my lips,*
rictumque in oris pervium	*and into the crossable gape of my mouth*
et labra pueri mollia	*and the soft lips of my boy*
rimata itineri transitus,	*burrowing a cross-passage for her journey,*
ut transiliret nititur.	*she struggles to leap across.*
Tum si morae quid plusculae	*Then, if there'd been some tiny bit*
fuisset in coetu osculi,	*more lingering in this kiss-hookup,*
amoris igni percita	*propelled by the fire of love*
transisset ut me linqueret	*she'd have crossed, so she might leave me;*
et—mira prorsum res foret—	*and—an outright miraculous thing—*
ut fierem ad me mortuus,	*so I'd become dead to myself*
ad puerum et intus viverem.	*and, to my boy, and inside him, alive.*

Gellius presents this poem as inspired by a two-line poem in Greek by Plato about kissing Agathon. For Gellius's kiss-poem stories, see n. 2, letter 14. On the difference between *osculum* and *savium,* see the volume introduction. On Epicurean ideas about *imagines* and dreams, see n. 3 above.

18. your royal neck: Lat. *tuas cervices regias.* Fronto refers again to kissing Marcus's neck in letter 45. Usually, the concept *royal* has a negative meaning in Latin, something like "tyrannical"; it is not normally used of the emperors and their families.

Letter 45

To my Lord,

That *néologisme*[1] that's allowed to poets—making up new words so they can express more easily what they feel—this is what I need to show my happiness. No, I'm not content with ordinary, everyday words—that's how too insanely happy I am for me to be able to communicate the gladness in my heart in commonplace language, now that you've written me so many letters in so few days,[2] and letters composed so elegantly so lovingly[3] so sweetly so effusively so burningly, though you're scraped raw by so much business, so many duties, so many official letters you have to write to all the provinces. But that's why I'd made up my mind—after all, it's not right for me to keep any secrets from you or put up pretenses—well, so I'd made up my mind even to submit to charges of laziness from you because I was writing to you more rarely, rather than burden you with my letters when you're busy with so many things, and goad you into writing back that way—and now all by yourself you've written me daily. But why am I saying "daily"? Now here's where I need some *néologisme*. Because it would be "daily" if you'd written me one letter a day; but when there are actually more letters than days, this word "daily" doesn't mean enough. And there's no reason, Lord, why you should be cross with me just because I was really frightened that my letters would be a burden to you if they were too frequent: because the more loving you are to me, I ought to be that much more sparing of your labors, that much more respectful of the things that keep you busy.[4]

What is more delicious to me than your kiss?[5] That delicious scent,[6] that enjoyment, lies for me in your neck and your kiss. And yet the last time you were setting out, and your father[7] had already gotten into the wagon, and a crowd of people saying good-bye and kissing you thoroughly[8] was holding you back, it was better that I was the only one of all of them not to hug you or kiss you. Similarly in each and every other regard I of all people would never put what would be nice for me before your needs; in fact, if need be, I would buy you the lightest leisure with my heaviest labor and toil.

And so, thinking of how much work you deal with in writing letters, I'd made up my mind to address you more sparingly—and then you wrote me daily. When I got your letters, I suffered just what a lover[9] suffers who sees his darling[10] running toward him over a rough and dangerous road. For he's both glad to see him coming[11] toward him and afraid of the danger at the same time. That's why I don't like the play so popular among actors, where the loving girl waits for her loving young man by night,[12] with her lamp lit, standing in her tower while he's swimming in the sea. For I would rather be without you, although I burn with love for you, than let you swim so late at night in so deep a sea, lest the moon should set, lest the wind should put out the light, lest you should be seized there in the cold, lest the waves lest the shoals lest the fish somehow harm you.[13] This strategy[14] would be more becoming to a lover and better and more wholesome: not to pursue at the cost of another's deadly danger[15] the use of a pleasure[16] brief and to be regretted.

Now if I can turn from fiction to the truth, I was anxious about this in no small way, in case I'd be adding something annoying and burdensome on top of the work you have to do, if along with those letters that you write to so many people every day as part of your job, I was also harassing you to write back. After all, I'd rather lack all enjoyment of your love myself than have you undergo even the least bit of inconvenience for the sake of my pleasure.

Notes

1. *néologisme:* Gk. *onomatopoeia.* This figure of rhetoric is as Fronto defines it here; words that imitate sounds (the common meaning today) constitute only one type of onomatopoeia.

2. so many . . . days: Marcus has sent Fronto a series of letters (not extant).

3. lovingly: Lat. *amicissime.*

4. the more loving . . . busy: For the thought, contrast Marcus to Fronto in letter 12, where it is Marcus who worries about imposing on Fronto's busy day, Marcus who says the love he feels should remind him to respect Fronto—a thought Fronto may be echoing here, perhaps with some bitterness or melancholy.

5. kiss: As seen in this passage, Romans commonly greeted each other and

said good-bye with a kiss. But of course the kiss is also a common event in erotic poetry in Latin.

6. scent: The connection of scent with kisses belongs without ambiguity to the realm of erotic poetry (see, e.g., Martial 3.65, with discussion in Richlin 1992, 39–40).

7. father: Antoninus Pius, the emperor.

8. kissing . . . thoroughly: Lat. *exosculantium* (cf. n. 9, letter 44). As in letter 44, here this verb is ambiguously erotic, although we might well imagine good-bye kisses from people with a range of relationships with Marcus. Compare Pliny *Natural History* 11.146, *hos [oculos] cum exosculamur animum ipsum videmur attingere,* "When we kiss [*exosculamur*] the eyes, we seem to touch the soul itself."

9. lover: Lat. *amator,* the Latin equivalent of the word *erastês. Amator,* however, usually refers to a woman's male lover.

10. darling: Lat. *delicias;* this word was commonly used for adolescent boys as sex objects, or for pet child slaves (see Richlin 1992, 223), or for any beloved person or thing.

11. him coming: In Latin, this is expressed by a single word, the participle *advenientem,* which is gender neutral; it could also be translated as "the one coming."

12. the play . . . night: The story of Hero and Leander, in which Hero stands each night in her tower holding a lamp to guide her lover, Leander, as he swims the Hellespont to see her. Van den Hout (1999, 124–25) argues that Fronto is here speaking of the ballet rather than the play. The tale was the subject of a poem by Musaeus (fifth century CE). Helen Morales's arguments about the gendering of voice in Musaeus's poem are very suggestive for this letter; as she notes, in the story Hero and Leander are kept apart "by duty and the Hellespont," Hero being a priestess of Aphrodite (Morales 1999, 42).

13. For I . . . harm you: Some scholars believe that this is a quotation from a lost tragedy of the second century BCE, because of the high concentration of poetic and archaic words. But Marcus and Fronto usually attribute their quotations to an author; this passage is arguably the climax of the correspondence; and Fronto was a gifted writer with a taste for archaic language.

14. This strategy: Housman emended the text's *oratio,* "speech," to *ratio,* "strategy" (the word refers to what follows; cf. letters 8–10, 15, in which the term *ratio* comes up repeatedly).

15. deadly danger: Lat. *capitali periculo.* Compare letter 17 at n. 7, where Marcus says Fronto fills him with "death-penalty love," *amore capitali.* So "the cost of another's *capitali* danger" might mean "making someone risk execution." The phrase *capitali periculo* appears in *Rope,* a play by Plautus (*Rudens* 349), where it refers to the danger of death by drowning after a shipwreck, and it seems possible that, as in the earlier letter Marcus was quoting Naevius, so here Fronto may be

quoting Plautus. But maybe not. Although Fronto disliked Seneca, Seneca (*On the Brevity of Life* 10.15.1) provides a more thought-provoking parallel than Plautus: the classical Greek philosophers make good friends—"with none of *these* will conversation be dangerous [*periculosus*], with none of *these* will a friendship be deadly [*amicitia capitalis*]."

16. pleasure: Letters? Something else?

Letter 46

To my Lord,

Whatever you have prayed for me, it all depends on your own well-being. My own sanity, good health, happiness, and good times are there, when you enjoy a body, mind, and reputation so undamaged—you who are so dear to your father, so sweet to your mother, so consecrated to your wife,[1] so good and kind to your brother. These are the things that make me want to live, ill as I am. Away from you, enough and to spare[2] of age and work and art and fame, and truly somewhat more than enough and to spare of pain and sickness.

I gave my daughter[3] the kiss you bid me to. She never seemed to me so sweet and so well kissed.[4] Say hello to your Lady, sweetest Lord. Good-bye and take a kiss to your little madam.[5]

Notes

1. wife: Faustina the Younger. Note that Fronto avoids an emotive adjective in Faustina's case.

2. enough and to spare: The same phrase appears at Catullus 7.2, there describing kisses; perhaps Fronto is again echoing Catullus here. But the phrase is not uncommon.

3. daughter: Fronto's daughter Cratia, who would now be about six years old.

4. well kissed: Lat. *saviata,* a verb formed from *savium.* On words for kissing, see the volume introduction.

5. your little madam: Lat. *matronae tuae; matrona* = "respectable married woman." This seems to refer to Marcus's first baby girl; this use of *matrona* shows up again in another letter (Haines 1.244–45 = *M. Caes.* 5.42 [57] = van den Hout, p. 81, line 27), where it is clearly a pet name for small girls (see also Haines 1.188–89 = *M. Caes.* 4.10 = van den Hout, p. 64, line 24). It is not a usual way to speak to a man of his wife.

Concordance

This concordance serves two sets of readers. The general reader may wish to find the letters in this collection in Haines's Loeb translation, where they can be seen in the context of the Fronto letter collection as a whole. Classicists will want to see the original text, but not every library will own all the main editions of Fronto, and unfortunately they all use different numbering systems, while Champlin's 1980 biography of Fronto uses yet another. The concordance should enable readers to find at least one version to compare with this one.

References are (in order): to volume and page number in Haines's Loeb edition of 1919–20, to book/item number in Naber's edition of 1867, to page number and book/item number in van den Hout's 1988 Teubner edition, and to book/item number in Champlin 1980, appendix A, explanations for which are provided in Champlin 1974. Haines uses Naber's book/item numbers; van den Hout makes changes to Naber's numbers. The book/item numbers in van den Hout 1988 and Champlin 1980 agree in most but not all cases, because Champlin was referring to the numbering used in an edition van den Hout produced in 1954 that was superseded by the 1988 edition. Naber's edition has book/item numbers but no section numbers within letters; Haines adds section numbers, as does van den Hout, but different ones. In van den Hout's commentary (1999), notes are numbered only according to the *page numbers* in his Teubner text, so the only practical way to use the commentary is with that text, which does include a concordance to Haines's translation at the very end (1988, 295–96). The Teubner also includes a useful collection of all Fronto's testimonia (places where other ancient writers talk about him; 1988, 259–76). The Haines Loeb contains the only complete translation of all the Fronto letters into English.

The book/item numbers follow the convention of the ancient edition as transmitted in the manuscripts, in that the collection is divided up into "books" with separate titles, with each item in the book numbered consecutively. Some titles, however, are produced by modern editors; modern titles for the Fronto books are not consistent. Abbreviations appearing below are as follows:

M. Caes. = *Ad Marcum Caesarem* (*To Marcus Caesar*)
Epist. Graec. = *Epistulae Graecae* (*Greek Letters*), Naber
Ep. Var. = *Epistulae Variae* (*Various Letters*), Champlin
Addit. = *Additamentum Epistularum Variarum Acephalum* (*Untitled Appendix with Various Letters*), van den Hout

Letter 1 (M to F) = Haines 1.18–21 = *Epist. Graec.* 6 = van den Hout, p. 42, *M. Caes.* 3.9 = Champlin *M. Caes.* 3.9
Letter 2 (F to M) = Haines 1.20–31 = *Epist. Graec.* 8 = van den Hout, pp. 250–55, *Addit.* 8 = Champlin *Ep. Var.* 8
Letter 3 (M to F) = Haines 1.30–33 = *Epist. Graec.* 7 = van den Hout, pp. 249–50, *Addit.* 7 = Champlin *Ep. Var.* 7
Letter 4 (M to F) = Haines 1.32–35 = *M. Caes.* 3.7 = van den Hout, p. 40, *M. Caes.* 3.7 = Champlin *M. Caes.* 3.7
Letter 5 (M to F) = Haines 1.50–51 = *M. Caes.* 3.9 = van den Hout, p. 43, *M. Caes.* 3.10 = Champlin *M. Caes.* 3.10
Letter 6 (F to M) = Haines 1.52–53 = *M. Caes.* 3.10 = van den Hout, p. 43, *M. Caes.* 3.11 = Champlin *M. Caes.* 3.11
Letter 7 (M to F) = Haines 1.52–55 = *M. Caes.* 5.59 [74] = van den Hout, p. 85, *M. Caes.* 5.74 = Champlin *M. Caes.* 5.74
Letter 8 (M to F) = Haines 1.58–63 = *M. Caes.* 3.2 = van den Hout, p. 36, *M. Caes.* 3.2 = Champlin *M. Caes.* 3.2
Letter 9 (F to M) = Haines 1.62–67 = *M. Caes.* 3.3 = van den Hout, pp. 36–38, *M. Caes.* 3.3 = Champlin *M. Caes.* 3.3
Letter 10 (M to F) = Haines 1.66–69 = *M. Caes.* 3.5 = van den Hout, p. 38, *M. Caes.* 3.5 = Champlin *M. Caes.* 3.5
Letter 11 (F to M) = Haines 1.70–75 = *M. Caes.* 4.1 = van den Hout, pp. 53–54, *M. Caes.* 4.1 = Champlin *M. Caes.* 4.1
Letter 12 (M to F) = Haines 1.74–79 = *M. Caes.* 4.2 = van den Hout, pp. 54–56, *M. Caes.* 4.2 = Champlin *M. Caes.* 4.2
Letter 13 (M to F) = Haines 1.78–81 = *M. Caes.* 3.18 = van den Hout, p. 51, *M. Caes.* 3.19 = Champlin *M. Caes.* 3.19
Letter 14 (M to F) = Haines 1.80–83 = *M. Caes.* 1.2 = van den Hout, pp. 1–2, *M. Caes.* 1.2 = Champlin *M. Caes.* 1.2
Letter 15 (F to M) = Haines 1.82–91 = *M. Caes.* 1.3 = van den Hout, pp. 2–5, *M. Caes.* 1.3 = Champlin *M. Caes.* 1.3

Letter 16 (M to F) = Haines 1.106–9 = *M. Caes.* 3.17 = van den Hout, p. 50,
  M. Caes. 3.18 = Champlin *M. Caes.* 3.18
Letter 17 (M to F) = Haines 1.112–15 = *M. Caes.* 2.2 = van den Hout, pp. 25–26,
  M. Caes. 2.5 = Champlin *M. Caes.* 2.2
Letter 18 (M to F) = Haines 1.116–17 = *M. Caes.* 2.4 = van den Hout, p. 28,
  M. Caes. 2.7 = Champlin *M. Caes.* 2.4
Letter 19 (M to F) = Haines 1.116–19 = *M. Caes.* 2.5 = van den Hout, pp. 29–30,
  M. Caes. 2.10 = Champlin *M. Caes.* 2.7
Letter 20 (F to M) = Haines 1.118–25 = *M. Caes.* 1.8 = van den Hout, pp. 17–21,
  M. Caes. 2.2 = Champlin *M. Caes.* 1.9
Letter 21 (F to Domitia Lucilla) = Haines 1.130–37 = *Epist. Graec.* 1 = van den
  Hout, pp. 21–24, *M. Caes.* 2.3 = Champlin *M. Caes.* 1.10
Letter 22 (M to F) = Haines 1.136–41 = *M. Caes.* 2.10 = van den Hout, pp. 28–
  29, *M. Caes.* 2.8 = Champlin *M. Caes.* 2.5
Letter 23 (M to F) = Haines 1.128–31 = *M. Caes.* 2.3 = van den Hout, p. 27,
  M. Caes. 2.6 = Champlin *M. Caes.* 2.3
Letter 24 (F to M) = Haines 1.144–45 = *M. Caes.* 2.7 = van den Hout, p. 31,
  M. Caes. 2.12 = Champlin *M. Caes.* 2.9
Letter 25 (M to F) = Haines 1.140–45 = *M. Caes.* 2.6 = van den Hout, pp. 30–31,
  M. Caes. 2.11 = Champlin *M. Caes.* 2.8
Letter 26 (F to M) = Haines 1.144–47 = *M. Caes.* 2.8 = van den Hout, p. 32,
  M. Caes. 2.13 = Champlin *M. Caes.* 2.10
Letter 27 (M to F) = Haines 1.152–53 = *M. Caes.* 2.13 = van den Hout, pp. 34–35,
  M. Caes. 2.17 = Champlin *M. Caes.* 2.14
Letter 28 (M to F) = Haines 1.170–71 = *M. Caes.* 3.19 = van den Hout, p. 51,
  M. Caes. 3.20 = Champlin *M. Caes.* 3.20
Letter 29 (M to F) = Haines 1.192–93 = *M. Caes.* 5.5 [20] = van den Hout,
  pp. 71–72, *M. Caes.* 5.20 = Champlin *M. Caes.* 5.20
Letter 30 (M to F) = Haines 1.152–55 = *M. Caes.* 2.14 = van den Hout, p. 35,
  M. Caes. 2.18 = Champlin *M. Caes.* 2.15
Letter 31 (M to F) = Haines 1.172–75 = *M. Caes.* 3.21 = van den Hout, p. 52,
  M. Caes. 3.22 = Champlin *M. Caes.* 3.22
Letter 32 (M to F) = Haines 1.154–63 = *M. Caes.* 1.6 = van den Hout, pp. 10–13,
  M. Caes. 1.6 = Champlin *M. Caes.* 1.6
Letter 33 (F to M) = Haines 1.162–69 = *M. Caes.* 1.7 = van den Hout, pp. 13–16,
  M. Caes. 1.7 = Champlin *M. Caes.* 1.7
Letter 34 (F to Herodes Atticus) = Haines 1.168–71 = *Epist. Graec.* 3 = van den
  Hout, pp. 16–17, *M. Caes.* 2.1 = Champlin *M. Caes.* 1.8
Letter 35 (M to F) = Haines 1.150–53 = *M. Caes.* 2.12 = van den Hout, p. 34,
  M. Caes. 2.16 = Champlin *M. Caes.* 2.13

Letter 36 (F to M) = Haines 1.172–73 = *M. Caes.* 3.20 = van den Hout, p. 51, *M. Caes.* 3.21 = Champlin *M. Caes.* 3.21

Letter 37 (M to F) = Haines 1.174–77 = *M. Caes.* 4.4 = van den Hout, pp. 60–61, *M. Caes.* 4.4 = Champlin *M. Caes.* 4.4

Letter 38 (M to F) = Haines 1.178–81 = *M. Caes.* 4.5 = van den Hout, pp. 61–62, *M. Caes.* 4.5 = Champlin *M. Caes.* 4.5

Letter 39 (M to F) = Haines 1.180–83 = *M. Caes.* 4.6 = van den Hout, pp. 62–63, *M. Caes.* 4.6 = Champlin *M. Caes.* 4.6

Letter 40 (M to F) = Haines 1.184–85 = *M. Caes.* 4.7 = van den Hout, p. 63, *M. Caes.* 4.7 = Champlin *M. Caes.* 4.7

Letter 41 (F to M) = Haines 1.186–89 = *M. Caes.* 4.9 = van den Hout, p. 64, *M. Caes.* 4.9 = Champlin *M. Caes.* 4.9

Letter 42 (M to F) = Haines 1.214–19 = *M. Caes.* 4.13 = van den Hout, pp. 67–68, *M. Caes.* 4.13 = Champlin *M. Caes.* 4.13

Letter 43 (F to M) = Haines 1.218–19 = *M. Caes.* 5.29 [44] = van den Hout, p. 77, *M. Caes.* 5.44 = Champlin *M. Caes.* 5.44

Letter 44 (F to M) = Haines 1.202–9 = *M. Caes.* 4.12 = van den Hout, pp. 65–67, *M. Caes.* 4.12 = Champlin *M. Caes.* 4.12

Letter 45 (F to M) = Haines 1.218–23 = *M. Caes.* 3.13 = van den Hout, pp. 45–47, *M. Caes.* 3.14 = Champlin *M. Caes.* 3.14

Letter 46 (F to M) = Haines 1.232–33 = *M. Caes.* 5.33 [48] = van den Hout, p. 78, *M. Caes.* 5.48 = Champlin *M. Caes.* 5.48

Works Cited

Adams, James Eli. 1995. *Dandies and Desert Saints: Styles of Victorian Manhood.* Ithaca, NY: Cornell University Press.

Altman, Janet Gurkin. 1982. *Epistolarity: Approaches to a Form.* Columbus: Ohio State University Press.

Ando, Clifford. 2000. *Imperial Ideology and Provincial Loyalty in the Roman Empire.* Berkeley and Los Angeles: University of California Press.

Bagnall, Roger S., and Raffaella Cribiore. 2005. *Women's Letters from Ancient Egypt, 300 BC–AD 800.* Ann Arbor: University of Michigan Press.

Beard, Mary. 2002. "Ciceronian Correspondences: Making a Book out of Letters." In *Classics in Progress,* ed. T. P. Wiseman, 103–44. Oxford: Oxford University Press.

Benner, Allen Rogers, and Francis H. Fobes, trans. 1949. *The Letters of Alkiphron, Aelian and Philostratus.* Cambridge, MA: Harvard University Press.

Birley, Anthony. 1987. *Marcus Aurelius: A Biography.* Rev. ed. London: B. T. Batsford.

———, trans. 1976. *Lives of the Later Caesars.* Harmondsworth: Penguin.

Boswell, John. 1980. *Christianity, Social Tolerance, and Homosexuality: Gay People in Western Europe from the Beginning of the Christian Era to the Fourteenth Century.* Chicago: University of Chicago Press.

Boughner, Robert. 1990. "The Sex Life of Marcus Aurelius." Paper presented at the annual meeting of the American Philological Association, San Francisco, December 30.

Bowman, Alan K. 1994. *Life and Letters on the Roman Frontier: Vindolanda and Its People.* London: British Museum Press.

Bray, Alan. 2003. *The Friend.* Chicago: University of Chicago Press.

Bristow, Joseph. 1995. *Effeminate England: Homoerotic Writing after 1885.* New York: Columbia University Press.

Brock, M. Dorothy. 1911. *Studies in Fronto and His Age.* Cambridge: Cambridge University Press.

Brooten, Bernadette. 1996. *Love between Women: Early Christian Responses to Female Homoeroticism.* Chicago: University of Chicago Press.

Butler, Shane. 2002. *The Hand of Cicero.* London: Routledge.

Carpenter, Edward, ed. 1902. *Ioläus: An Anthology of Friendship.* Manchester: S. Clarke.

Cassan, Armand, ed. and trans. 1830. *Lettres inédites de Marc-Aurèle et de Fronton.* 2 vols. Paris: A. Levavasseur.

Champlin, Edward. 1980. *Fronto and Antonine Rome.* Cambridge, MA: Harvard University Press.

———. 1974. "The Chronology of Fronto." *Journal of Roman Studies* 64:136–59.

Clarke, John R. 1998. *Looking at Lovemaking: Constructions of Sexuality in Roman Art, 100 B.C.–A.D. 250.* Berkeley and Los Angeles: University of California Press.

Collier, Jeremy, ed. and trans. 1701. *The Emperor Marcus Antoninus His Conversation with Himself.* London: Richard Sare.

Costa, C. D. N., ed. 2001. *Greek Fictional Letters.* Oxford: Oxford University Press.

Courtney, Edward. 1993. *The Fragmentary Latin Poets.* Oxford: Clarendon.

Crook, John. 1967. *Law and Life of Rome.* Ithaca, NY: Cornell University Press.

Davidson, James. 2001. "Dover, Foucault and Greek Homosexuality: Penetration and the Truth of Sex." *Past and Present* 170:3–51.

———. 1997. *Courtesans and Fishcakes.* London: HarperCollins.

Dixon, Suzanne. 1997. "Continuity and Change in Roman Social History: Retrieving 'Family Feeling(s)' from Roman Law and Literature." In *Inventing Ancient Culture,* ed. Mark Golden and Peter Toohey, 79–90. London: Routledge.

Dover, K. J. 1978. *Greek Homosexuality.* 2nd ed. Cambridge, MA: Harvard University Press.

Dowling, Linda. 1994. *Hellenism and Homosexuality in Victorian Oxford.* Ithaca, NY: Cornell University Press.

Ebbeler, Jennifer Valerie. 2002. "Pedants in the Apparel of Heroes? Cultures of Latin Letter-Writing from Cicero to Ennodius." Ph.D. diss., University of Pennsylvania.

Faderman, Lillian. 1998. *Surpassing the Love of Men: Romantic Friendship and Love between Women from the Renaissance to the Present.* New York: William Morrow.

Farrar, F. W. 1874. *Seekers after God.* London: Macmillan.

Fleury, Pascale, and Ségolène Demougin, eds. and trans. 2003. *Fronton: Correspondance.* Paris: Belles Lettres.

Flower, Harriet I. 2000. *Ancestor Masks and Aristocratic Power in Roman Culture.* Oxford: Oxford University Press.

Foucault, Michel. 1988. *The Care of the Self.* Translated by Robert Hurley. New York: Viking.

Gaca, Kathy L. 2003. *The Making of Fornication: Eros, Ethics, and Political Reform in Greek Philosophy and Early Christianity.* Berkeley and Los Angeles: University of California Press.

Gleason, Maud W. 1995. *Making Men: Sophists and Self-Presentation in Ancient Rome.* Princeton, NJ: Princeton University Press.

Gunderson, Erik. 1997. "Catullus, Pliny, and Love-Letters." *Transactions of the American Philological Association* 127:201–31.

Habinek, Thomas N. 1998. *The Politics of Latin Literature.* Princeton, NJ: Princeton University Press.

Haines, C. R., ed. and trans. 1919–20. *The Correspondence of Marcus Cornelius Fronto.* 2 vols. London: William Heinemann.

Hallett, Judith P., and Marilyn B. Skinner, eds. 1997. *Roman Sexualities.* Princeton, NJ: Princeton University Press.

Halperin, David M. 1992. "Historicizing the Sexual Body: Sexual Preferences and Erotic Identities in the Pseudo-Lucianic *Erotes.*" In *Discourses of Sexuality,* ed. Domna C. Stanton, 236–61. Ann Arbor: University of Michigan Press.

———. 1990. *One Hundred Years of Homosexuality.* New York: Routledge.

Hansen, Karen V. 1992. "'Our Eyes Behold Each Other': Masculinity and Intimate Friendship in Antebellum New England." In *Men's Friendships,* ed. Peter M. Nardi, 35–58. Newbury Park, CA: Sage.

Harris, William V. 1989. *Ancient Literacy.* Cambridge, MA: Harvard University Press.

Henderson, Jeffrey. 1991. *The Maculate Muse.* Rev. ed. Oxford: Oxford University Press.

Holford-Strevens, Leofranc. 1988. *Aulus Gellius.* Chapel Hill: University of North Carolina Press.

Hubbard, Thomas K. 2005. "Pindar's *Tenth Olympian* and Athlete-Trainer Pederasty." *Journal of Homosexuality* 49, nos. 3–4: 137–71.

———. 2003. *Homosexuality in Greece and Rome: A Sourcebook of Basic Documents.* Berkeley and Los Angeles: University of California Press.

———. 1998. "Popular Perceptions of Elite Homosexuality in Classical Athens." *Arion* 6, no. 1: 48–78.

Hunt, A. S., and C. C. Edgar, eds. and trans. 1932. *Non-literary Papyri.* Vol. 1 of *Select Papyri.* London: William Heinemann.

Inman, B. A. 1991. "Estrangement and Connection: Walter Pater, Benjamin Jowett, and William M. Hardinge." In *Pater in the 1990s,* ed. Laurel Brake and Ian Small, 1–20. Greensboro, NC: ELT Press.

Johnson, Samuel. 1756. *A Dictionary of the English Language.* 2 vols. London: J. Knapton et al.

Konstan, David. 2002. "Enacting *Eros.*" In *The Sleep of Reason,* ed. Martha C. Nussbaum and Juha Sihvola, 354–73. Chicago: University of Chicago Press.

———. 1997. *Friendship in the Classical World.* Cambridge: Cambridge University Press.

Larmour, David H. J., Paul Allen Miller, and Charles Platter, eds. 1998. *Rethinking Sexuality: Foucault and Classical Antiquity.* Princeton, NJ: Princeton University Press.

Long, George, trans. 1887. *The Thoughts of the Emperor M. Aurelius Antoninus.* London: George Bell & Sons.

Macfait, Ebenezer. 1760. *Remarks on the Life and Writings of Plato.* Edinburgh: A. Millar et al.

MacMullen, Ramsay. 1974. *Roman Social Relations.* New Haven, CT: Yale University Press.

Magie, David, trans. 1921. *Historia Augusta.* Vol. 1. Cambridge, MA: Harvard University Press.

Marchand, Suzanne L. 1996. *Down from Olympus: Archaeology and Philhellenism in Germany, 1750–1970.* Princeton, NJ: Princeton University Press.

Mattingly, Harold. 1940. *Coins of the Roman Empire in the British Museum.* Vol. 4. London: British Museum.

Mayor, John E. B., ed. 1877–78. *Thirteen Satires of Juvenal.* London: Macmillan.

McQuige, J. 1824. *Selections from Fronto's Letters.* Rome: Alessandro Caracchi.

Montserrat, Dominic. 1996. *Sex and Society in Graeco-Roman Egypt.* London: Kegan Paul.

Morales, Helen. 1999. "Gender and Identity in Musaeus' *Hero and Leander.*" In *Constructing Identities in Late Antiquity,* ed. Richard Miles, 41–69. London: Routledge.

Morris, Edward P., ed. 1909. *Horace: The Satires.* New York: American Book Company.

Naber, Samuel Adrianus, ed. 1867. *M. Cornelii Frontonis et M. Aurelii Imperatoris Epistulae.* Leipzig: Teubner.

Nehamas, Alexander, and Paul Woodruff, trans. 1995. *Plato* Phaedrus. Indianapolis: Hackett.

Niebuhr, B. G. 1843. "Über die zu Mailand entdeckten Schriften des M. Cor-

nelius Fronto." In *Kleine historische und philologische Schriften*, 2:52–72.
Bonn: Eduard Weber. [Original date of publication given as 1816.]

Norton, Rictor. 1997. *The John Addington Symonds Pages*.
http://www.infopt.demon.co.uk/symindex.htm.

Oliensis, Ellen. 1997. "The Erotics of *Amicitia:* Readings in Tibullus, Propertius, and Horace." In *Roman Sexualities,* ed. Judith P. Hallett and Marilyn
B. Skinner, 151–71. Princeton, NJ: Princeton University Press.

Pater, Walter. 1885. *Marius the Epicurean.* London: Macmillan.

———. 1873. *Studies in the History of the Renaissance.* London: Macmillan.

Perkins, Judith. 1995. *The Suffering Self: Pain and Narrative Representation in
the Early Christian Era.* London: Routledge.

Portalupi, Felicità, ed. and trans. 1974. *Opere di Marco Cornelio Frontone.*
Turin: Unione Tipografico-Editrice Torinese.

Prins, Yopie. 1999. *Victorian Sappho.* Princeton, NJ: Princeton University Press.

Reardon, B. P., ed. 1989. *Collected Ancient Greek Novels.* Berkeley and Los
Angeles: University of California Press.

Reynolds, L. D., and N. G. Wilson. 1974. *Scribes and Scholars.* 2nd ed. Oxford:
Oxford University Press.

Richlin, Amy. 2005. "Eros Underground: Greece and Rome in Gay Print Culture, 1953–65." *Journal of Homosexuality* 49, nos. 3–4: 421–61.

———. 2001. "Emotional Work: Lamenting the Roman Dead." In *Essays in
Honor of Gordon Williams: Twenty-five Years at Yale,* ed. Elizabeth Tylawsky
and Charles Weiss, 229–48. New Haven, CT: Henry R. Schwab.

———. 1999. "Cicero's Head." In *Constructions of the Classical Body,* ed. James
I. Porter, 190–211. Ann Arbor: University of Michigan Press.

———. 1997. "Rhetoric and Gender." In *Roman Persuasion,* ed. William
Dominik, 90–110. London: Routledge.

———. 1996. "How Putting the Man in Roman Put the Roman in Romance."
In *Talking Gender: Public Images, Personal Journeys, and Political Critiques,*
ed. Nancy Hewitt, Jean O'Barr, and Nancy Rosebaugh, 14–35. Chapel Hill:
University of North Carolina Press.

———. 1993. "Not before Homosexuality: The Materiality of the *Cinaedus*
and the Roman Law against Love between Men." *Journal of the History of
Sexuality* 3, no. 4: 523–73.

———. 1992. *The Garden of Priapus.* Rev. ed. New York: Oxford University
Press.

Rosenmeyer, Patricia A. 2001. *Ancient Epistolary Fictions: The Letter in Greek
Literature.* Cambridge: Cambridge University Press.

Rowlandson, Jane, ed. 1998. *Women and Society in Greek and Roman Egypt: A
Sourcebook.* Cambridge: Cambridge University Press.

Ruden, Sarah, trans. 2000. *Petronius* Satyricon. Indianapolis: Hackett.

Sedgwick, Eve Kosofsky. 1992. *Between Men: English Literature and Male Homosocial Desire.* 2nd ed. New York: Columbia University Press.

Skinner, Marilyn B. 2005. *Sexuality in Greek and Roman Culture.* Oxford: Blackwell.

Stewart, Susan. 1984. *On Longing.* Baltimore: Johns Hopkins University Press.

Trapp, M. B. 1990. "Plato's *Phaedrus* in Second-Century Greek Literature." In *Antonine Literature,* ed. D. A. Russell, 141–73. Oxford: Clarendon Press.

Trapp, Michael, ed. 2003. *Greek and Latin Letters: An Anthology, with Translation.* Cambridge: Cambridge University Press.

van den Hout, Michael P. J. 1999. *A Commentary on the Letters of M. Cornelius Fronto.* Leiden: Brill.

———. 1988. *M. Cornelius Fronto Epistulae.* Leipzig: Teubner.

Walters, Jonathan. 1993. "'No More Than a Boy': The Shifting Construction of Masculinity from Ancient Greece to the Middle Ages." *Gender and History* 5, no. 1: 20–33.

Williams, Craig. 1999. *Homosexuality and the Roman Man.* Oxford: Oxford University Press.

Winkler, John J. 1990. *The Constraints of Desire.* New York: Routledge.

———, trans. 1989. "Leucippe and Clitophon." In *Collected Ancient Greek Novels,* ed. B. P. Reardon, 170–284. Berkeley and Los Angeles: University of California Press.

The Works of Plato Abridg'd. 1701. London: A. Bell.

Wright, Wilmer Cave, trans. 1952. *Philostratus and Eunapius: The Lives of the Sophists.* Cambridge, MA: Harvard University Press.

Zetzel, James E. G. 2000. Review of *A Commentary on the Letters of M. Cornelius Fronto,* by Michael P. J. van den Hout (1999). *Bryn Mawr Classical Review,* July 26. Available at http://ccat.sas.upenn.edu/bmcr/2000/2000–07–26.html.

———. 1980. "The Subscriptions in the Manuscripts of Livy and Fronto and the Meaning of *Emendatio.*" *Classical Philology* 75:38–59.

———. 1973. "*Emendavi ad Tironem:* Some Notes on Scholarship in the Second Century A.D." *Harvard Studies in Classical Philology* 77:227–45.

Index

Catullus, Gaius Valerius (*continued*)
13, 78; poems as intertext for
Marcus-Fronto letters, 12, 27, 43,
53, 61, 109, 133, 142, 146, 152
Catulus, Quintus Lutatius, 69
Champlin, Edward, 4, 21, 22, 28, 35,
58, 140, 141
children, elite Roman: hitting, 144;
parents' feelings at death of, 17, 117,
123–24, 143; reared by slaves, 43
Cicero, Marcus Tullius, 53; death of,
9; as homework for Marcus, 52,
139; letters, diction of, 26, 98, 125;
letters, model for later writers, 5,
87; letters, publication of, 20, 22;
letters, to women, 27, 92, 137; letters, translated, 27; as model for
style, 119; as philosopher, 130, 145;
relationship with Tiro, 12–13; as
rhetorician, 14–15, 25, 42, 46, 88,
116, 120, 128; sexuality attacked, 16–
17; villa, 105
cinaedus (pl. *cinaedi*), 11, 66. See also
mollis
Clarke, John, 29, 73
class: free birth as virtue, 73, 81, 82,
146; Fronto patronizes Horace, 87–
88; lower-class food, 118, 120; Marcus looks down on rustics, 125, 126,
131, 134, 135–36
code, 7, 14, 17, 27, 70–72, 73, 95, 98,
104. *See also* food imagery; phallic
imagery
codex, definition of, 1
coins, 89
Commodus, 5, 9, 18
Cratia (daughter of Fronto), 17, 85,
108, 134, 144, 146, 152
Cratia (wife of Fronto), 17, 18, 77, 92,
106, 108, 110, 134
cruising, 73

Davidson, James, 11, 29, 41
devotio, 72
Domitia Lucilla, 4; addressed by
Fronto, 85, 90–95; friend of Cratia,
106, 110, 134; jealous of Fronto, 70.
See also Marcus Aurelius, relation-
ship with mother
Dover, K. J., 10, 29, 41, 120
Dowling, Linda, 6, 16, 30

Ebbeler, Jennifer, 5
editors, ancient, 121–22
effeminacy. See *mollis*
Ennius, Quintus, 64, 65, 82, 96, 97, 119,
121; *Annals,* 144, 146; *Sota,* 65, 66
erastês / erômenos (pl. *erastai / erômenoi*),
10, 13, 18, 40, 41, 45, 46, 47, 69, 94,
120, 140; *erastês* compared with
amator, 150
erôs, 94, 124
erôtikos logos. See Plato, *Phaedrus*
excerpting, 67, 96, 98

Faderman, Lillian, 6, 30
Faustina (daughter of Marcus Aurelius), 19, 143, 145, 152
Faustina (wife of Marcus Aurelius),
18, 141, 152
female homoerotic relationships, 10, 29
food imagery, 106, 118, 119, 120, 129–
30, 134
forgeries, 5, 122
Foucault, Michel, 10, 19, 29, 100
friends and friendship: ancient, 29,
40, 73, 78, 151; Cicero's, 20, 27;
Fronto's, 20, 93, 144; Marcus-
Fronto, 65, 71, 77, 138; sentimental,
6, 27, 40, 78
Fronto, Marcus Cornelius: appearance, 64–65; biography, 4, 22, 28,
58; brother, 65, 66, 102; children, 17

(see also Cratia [daughter of Fronto]); consulship, 77, 78, 107, 118, 119; education, 15, 123, 124, 143; ethnicity, 4, 36, 40, 58, 85, 89, 91, 92, 93, 95; friends, 20; house, 46, 84, 88; marriage, 17 (see also Cratia [wife of Fronto]); as orator, 75, 83; power imbalance with Marcus Aurelius, 43, 47, 56, 57, 58, 60, 69, 73, 75, 102, 115, 117, 122; speech on provincial wills, 113–17; speech praising Antoninus Pius, 77, 79, 90–95, 99–101, 104; style, 8, 24–26, 41, 53, 73, 86, 87, 98, 100, 116, 124, 146; as teacher, 15, 65, 99; use of similes, 41, 90–95, 116, 143, 145. See also rhetoric, Fronto on

Gaca, Kathy, 8, 16, 17, 29, 73
gay history, 6–7
Gellius, Aulus, 22, 26, 28, 69, 132, 146, 147
Gladiator, 5
Gleason, Maud, 14, 28, 81
Goldhill, Simon, 41
Gracchus, Gaius Sempronius, 65, 66, 67, 119, 121
Greek, writing in, 18, 25, 33, 85, 92, 103
Gunderson, Erik, 5

Hadrian, 4, 7, 9, 10, 57, 105
Haines, C. R.: chronology of letters, 21; comments, 41, 67, 88; as Loeb editor of Fronto and Marcus, 3; text, 23, 63; as translator, 24, 89, 97, 98, 124, 140
Hallett, Judith P., 29
Halperin, David, 10, 12, 29
Hauler, Edmund, 2
Henderson, Jeffrey, 29, 43, 132

Hercules, 119, 120
Hero and Leander, 149, 150
Herodes Atticus, 55; as consul, 107; and Domitia Lucilla, 55, 92; as Fronto's *anterastês*, 13, 123–24; loses son, 115, 117, 122, 123–24; as Marcus's teacher, 117, 123–24; as rhetorician, 81; on trial, 55, 56–59, 64, 65
Historia Augusta, 4–5, 18, 28
Holford-Strevens, Leofranc, 28, 69, 92, 117
homework. *See* pedagogy
homosexuality, male. *See* Achilles and Patroclus; *anterastês;* body, and wrestling; Catullus, Gaius Valerius; Catulus, Quintus Lutatius; *cinaedus;* code; cruising; Ennius, Quintus, *Sota; erastês/erômenos;* gay history; homosociality; Hyacinthus; invective; Jowett, Benjamin; Juvenal; *kinaidos;* kissing; love; love poetry; Lucian; Maecenas; male homoerotic relationships; *mollis;* Orpheus; *paidika;* pederasty; phallic imagery; Philostratus (erotic writer); plane trees; Plato; prostitution; sex; sex/gender system; Socrates; Strato; Symonds, John Addington; Tiro, Marcus Tullius; transgender analogies; Whitman, Walt
homosociality: in Roman education, 15; and writing, 12
Horace (Horatius Flaccus), 12, 13, 84, 87, 88, 97, 136
Hubbard, Thomas, 10, 11, 29, 41, 126
hunting, 46, 93, 127, 131
Hyacinthus, 43
hyena, 90, 92–93

illness. *See* body
imago (pl. *imagines*), 85–86, 145–46, 147

Inman, Billie, 7, 30
invective: ethnic, 57, 58, 125–26; in rhetoric, 42, 99; against sex between adult males, 11, 13, 42; verbal dueling, 134, 136; against younger partner in pederasty, 16, 42

Jews, 102
Jowett, Benjamin, 7, 15
Juvenal, 46, 58, 73, 87, 116, 117, 121, 125–26

kinaidos (pl. *kinaidoi*), 11, 13
kissing, 19; babies, 145, 152; in Catullus, 146; Domitia Lepida to Cratia, 106; Fronto to Marcus, 141, 144, 145, 148; as greeting, 148, 149–50; Marcus to Fronto, 99; poem about, in Gellius, 147; vocabulary for, 26, 89
Konstan, David, 18, 29, 78

Laberius, 86, 103, 104, 105, 119, 121
lameness, 68, 91, 94, 120, 140
law and lawyers: courtroom strategies, 127; Fronto in court, 33, 113–17; imagery based on, 147; invective against, 87, 105, 106, 131, 132; Marcus in court, 52, 111, 139; trial of Herodes Atticus, 54–60; wives of, 106
letters: circulation of, 20, 121; literary, 5, 27; by ordinary people, 27–28; production of, 21–22, 66, 85, 88, 137; theory of reading, 30
Liberalia, 63
Loeb Classical Library, 3
love: between friends, 62, 63, 65, 78; "death-penalty," 77, 78–79; Fronto's, for Marcus, 36–44, 57, 94, 123, 138, 144, 149; Marcus-Fronto, mutual, 63, 70–72, 75, 104, 118; Marcus's,

for Fronto, 33, 45, 49, 56, 64, 65, 67, 77, 103; of teachers, 123; toasting, 94; vocabulary for, 124. See also *erôs*
love poetry, 12–13, 23, 69, 73, 147, 150
Lucian, 43, 46, 87
Lysias, 35, 36, 39, 41, 46, 92

MacMullen, Ramsay, 126
Maecenas, 84, 88
magister, 25
Mai, Angelo, 1, 2, 3, 137
male homoerotic relationships, adult, 11, 58. See also *cinaedus; kinaidos; mollis*
Marchand, Suzanne, 29
Marcus Aurelius: biography, 4, 28, 63; brother (*see* Verus, Lucius); *Meditations* (*To Himself*), 3, 7–8, 23, 42, 50, 74, 124; misquotes literature, 75, 76, 78, 97, 132, 140; mother (*see* Domitia Lucilla); name, 4, 20, 34–35, 57, 81, 82, 86; relationship with mother, 4, 17–18, 34, 39, 43, 70, 77, 94, 110, 134, 135; as saint, 7; shifts in attitude toward Fronto, 49, 50, 67, 74, 75; souvenir images, 144, 147; style, 24–26, 46, 50, 53, 61, 66, 101, 126, 132, 135; writes in bed, 20, 48, 52, 131, 134, 135; writes poetry, 81, 82, 85, 88, 96, 131, 132
Marcus-Fronto letters: autograph, 21, 57, 59, 65, 66, 80, 96, 97, 116, 119, 122, 137, 138; chronology, 20–21; citations, 23; discovery, 1–3, 28; numbering system, 3, 30–31; reception, 13–14; as source of quotations from early Latin, 2; text, 23–24; themes (*see* body; class; code; hunting; kissing; lameness; love; prayers; shackles; sleep); translations, 3, 24, 27

CPSIA information can be obtained
at www.ICGtesting.com
Printed in the USA
LVHW03s0955140718
583472LV00005B/14/P